THE "A" WORDS

THE "A" WORDS

My Gut-Wrenching and Mildly Hilarious
Story From **A**buse and **A**bortion
Into Understanding Freedom

BY EMILY TURNER

THIS IS DEDICATED
TO MY GRANDPA JACK. A GREAT MAN
WHO HAS FOUGHT FOR OUR COUNTRY,
OUR FAMILY, HIS LIFE AND HIS BREATH WITH
ALS. A MAN WHO CONTINUES TO TEACH
ME THE VALUE AND GIFT OF THE FIGHT.

CONTENTS

The Opening **A**ddress   11

Section 1: Unfolding **A**buse
Chapter 1: I Plead My Case   21
Chapter 2: Coffee and Crumb Dust   37
Chapter 3: Crowns of Control   47
Chapter 4: Dirt Box and Da Bind Min   53
Chapter 5: Up-rooted in Un-forgiveness   61
Chapter 6: Mind the Traffick(ing)   71

Section 2: Uncovering **A**bortion
Chapter 7: Softness and Illumination   89
Chapter 8: Holy Berkeley, Batman   99
Chapter 9: The Flesh of Mercy   113
Chapter 10: Guts and Grit of PTSD   125
Chapter 11: A Bit Familiar   129
Chapter 12: My Ark   139
Chapter 13: Beyond the 'A'   151

Section 3: Letters of **A**bsolution

Chapter 14: To The Victors — 165

Chapter 15: To Those With An "A" In Their Story — 169

Chapter 16: To My Daughters — 173

An **A**fterward of Thoughts — 177

Appreciation — 183

Articles & **A**ids — 195

Archives — 189

About Me — 191

THE OPENING ADDRESS

*You will find comfort when God
takes your story to comfort others.
Lysa TerKeurst- It's Not Supposed To Be This Way*

It is an awe and wonder that you, my friend, are reading this. I am humbled (times a za-billion) that you have given your time for these stories. Thank you for sitting with me as I continue to grow and learn more of what God is doing here. Grab some Junior Mints, red wine, or banana bread and let's do this.

These are my stories, as I live and breathe. Stories that molded me and the heart beats of a God who loves me still. I say that because He does. He still loves me and sometimes we need to be reminded of that very truth. I hesitated with the subtitle, mainly because you may or may not be mildly offended by the *mildly hilarious* stories unfolding here. But as messy as this is, my story is also full of wild tales with the gift of humor and what a gift that is! I'm learning that this Defender, who gives us laughter and the perspective of wit, throws over the stones of injustice and pride, transgression and dismissal to expose both the tiniest and greatest of sins, pulling us out from the shards of darkness and walking with us into the light. It's a lesson I've toiled over most of my life- the idea that His love really is that great, that relentless, that understanding. Wonderfully patient, ferocious and perfect, providing boundaries as I search the lines of obedience and grace. He is all of what encompasses the greatest of Love. What He says about who He is, is in fact true, and I hope that these stories showcase how I've come to see that.

    As I've been editing this book for the three hundredth time (is a book ever, really finished or is time just up?), the kids have been back and forth between our backyard and a neighbor's house, running in semi-wet bathing suits and mismatched sandals while scarfing otter pops because it is one hundred and fifty percent summer time in the mountains. I laugh with them in their silly antics of making up wiggly arm dance moves to church camp songs from last month, or how they can't help but sing all the words wrong to the most famous Sir Mix-a-lot, Baby Got Back. Also, introducing Sir Mix-a-lot to my kids: Parenting win or not? Asking for a friend.

Shoes seem mostly optional at this point. Planned dinners, forget it. Here's to plates of salami, leftover gluten free noodles and whatever fruit we grabbed at Farmers Market. Here's to summer bathing in lakes or pools or the sprinklers. Wild hair and sunburned shoulders and the smell of day old sunscreen on the back of their necks. Summer time just sings of freedom and I'm clutched to the whole of it.

That kind of freedom, the captivating, gut-enthused, life-breathing and silly singing freedom is offered in abundance and it's here for you. Our stories and sins shouldn't hold us captive. There's more to them- more to us.

There's a word I heard once while I attended the church my folks go to. Aphesis, pronounced af'-es-is; it's the Greek word meaning freedom and release. I wrote it down as soon as I heard it and knew it would structure something for me. I played with the idea of giving this book that title, but none of my editing peers were sad to hear I didn't choose it. Good call, friends. Best not to have the eye squinting, cocked heads looking sideways at me when I say or they read the title.

Nevertheless, the word was immediately meaningful and it still is. A total release into freedom. What is better than living in the full, to the full? We are invited to know the God who sets us free because He invites us to. He holds a seat for you at the table of community and welcome. He greets you with grace. His flesh is your mercy. He chases you down amongst the flock and waves. He knows you by name, the greatest name of all- His. The God who is still parting wreckage and captivating the lost, prepares the path to wholeness. The God who knows our entire, wild story and loves us with triumph secures us. You and I are free to live our full story- the ugly and wretched and sorrowful; the wonder-filled and gentle, the mildly or dare I say wildly hilarious, because through Him and in Him, these stories spell redemption.

xo, *Emily*

SECTION 1: UNFOLDING **A**BUSE

CHAPTER ONE: I PLEAD MY CASE

My eleventh grade history teacher was a retired 6'6 forward for the Philadelphia 76'ers. As a nationally renowned athlete, his experience and title preceded him in many circles I'm sure, but I did not know that man. I didn't know his professional accolades or university record statistics. I didn't know when he was drafted or if he was the first or twentieth chosen. Much to my basketball and ESPN-obsessed friend, Sarah's dismay, I had never even planned an evening around any NBA game. Shocking, I know. Give me the 1990's 49er's roster with Joe Montana and Jerry Rice and I'd be singing a red and gold tune to the front of the class.

Though we had little in common, I knew the bald, stern and structured teacher who stood, paced and lectured dates and names I'd later and quickly forget. I knew the encouraging and sometimes silly man who'd sneak you a test answer or two if you caught him in the right mood on the right day. Regardless, at the beginning of every class period we were held to this one standard- put your backpack on the back of your seat. *Show me you're ready*, he'd often repeat. After asking one of the students numerous times to take his backpack off of the desk and *show me you're ready*, our teacher stood front and center and said (read: yelled; jury's still out on that one) we all failed for that day. This direct, corporal punishment seemed uncharacteristic of the otherwise patient and helpful teacher, but it was obvious in his tone and in his eyes, he was livid. And now, so was I. As were the twenty-two other students whose backpacks were slung over their seats with full attention. How could we all fail? What did this mean for our grades? I didn't know a teacher could do that. Could he? Why didn't this fool just put his backpack over his chair?

    From as young as I can remember, my mama would often comment that I argued as a lawyer. She'd roll her eyes at me and huff, or walk out of my bedroom mid-argument to save us both our lives, I'm sure. Some days I could really crawl under her skin when the situation called for it, like not getting to go to Great America unsupervised with my friends at thirteen years old. How dare she not trust the so obvious rebel pre-teen? I'd lawyer up, like she'd say, and that's exactly what I did for the remainder of the class period. In those next forty eight minutes, my notebook was full, cover to end with every reason why this particular corporal consequence was unjust. I argued and reasoned the larger percentage of respectful days we'd had over the year. Positive group project results. No blatant cheating on pop quizzes. Come on! Lists and notes and side notes covered pages that should have been taken up with details about who, what and why 1914 was important. When the bell rang for lunch, I approached the defendant's desk.

As calmly as my almost seventeen year old brain would muster and holding back the nervous cry, I walked him through my eighty six bullet points, mostly using professional and legal terms like, *it's not fair*. I was fearless and relentless, and surprised myself. He resembled nothing of my mother and yet I had the galls or gumption or ignorance, perhaps, to stand in the court. Most of the time I was so concerned with people liking me that it was both uncharacteristic yet freeing to let it fly. That day I pushed back and left his classroom reeling over the questions of how this could affect my grade and my reputation as his student. Would he tell other teachers? Would he see it as a matter of disrespect? Ever since Freshmen year, guidance counselors, coaches and teachers elevated the building up of Junior year. That year, we were told, mattered the most for college applications. It was the year of SAT prep. The year to balance out extracurriculars and build our case for college admissions. The year to stick with the said-necessary class and the also necessary after-school tutoring because math is from the devil. So here I was, nearing the end of this sacred and insane year, only to be caught in an ill-aimed failure.

I begrudgingly walked into class the next day partially embarrassed that I stood in the face of confrontation, but still holding ground I fully believed in as the teenage plaintiff. He sat, somber at his desk as the twenty four of us students piled into his classroom and took our seats. I didn't want to put my backpack on the chair that day. I didn't want to listen to anything this teacher had to say. I didn't want to look at the obnoxious guy who caused this as he walked in just after me and took his seat, somewhat kitty-corner to mine, backpack still on his desk. Just learn, bud. I wanted to yard sale my notebook and pens and textbook across my desk and on to the floor. Frustration clouded me but my better judgement convinced me to put the Jansport on my chair and let out the breath I'd been holding in. As our teacher stood just after the bell rang, pacing and verbally mapping out the structure of what would be that class period, he paused suddenly and took a seat on the edge of his oak desk, his glare at attention, mirroring ours. Without mentioning a name, he announced that because one student showed up for the rest of them, he wouldn't penalize the remaining class. I still couldn't make eye contact for fear that I'd give a tell and I wanted none of the attention. But you guys, I did it. He listened and for the first time in a long time, I believed in my words, believed in justice and was shown evidence that even the smallest details of our lives, like fighting for that B- in eleventh grade history, matter.

That was eighteen years ago. Sometimes I wonder why that's the story written so vividly in memory. Why, when sitting to write this book, it came first. You know what's funny, is that I didn't immediately tell my parents when that happened. There was something almost embarrassing about standing up to this man and I feared they'd see it as disrespect. Fast forward a few days after that class period to Friday night football at our high school's new field when I caught the intimidating glisten in the eyes of my parents talking with said teacher. *Oh crap.* I put my head down but the swarm of students couldn't hide me, beaming like a fluorescent pink disco ball in the middle of the darkest night, there I was. Deep breaths leveled me out and I faced them, wondering why they were laughing and smiling at me, calling me towards them with waving gestures. As I made my way down the metal bleachers, across the deep red track, dragging my feet towards them, I thought, *Maybe he didn't say anything about me. Maybe they were talking about another student's embarrassing approach.*

    I was wrong. *I was just telling your parents about you standing up to me the other day. You've sure made a mark.* The defendant rests.

    When I was ten, I was told no one would believe me. I didn't think I could ever stand up for myself. I believed then that my voice didn't matter. I was told that what was happening to me over those next few years was fine. I believed that my body was not mine to protect or to value. I believed that no one could protect me, not even God, and I grew to believe that myself and my story would always be broken. But when I was thirteen I stood unthreatened by my abuser. I told him then that it would stop and I told him a hundred times after. My words told him. My eyes told him. My hands told him. I was firm in my anger, firm in the idea that if he did it again, I would unleash a hundred thousand deafening screams to expose what he had done. He never touched me again but the scars he left were graves, deep and murky, filled with my bones that, as a young girl I was trying to piece back together somewhat functionally and mainly alone. There's no easy roadmap out from the darkness of molestation and I spent years in the silence of it, wading through isolation and the belief that even if I shared no one would care enough to help me reassemble myself.

In my thirty five years I've probably had close to one hundred mentors. Some I know by way of books. Others I know and learn from by their social media outlets. Many I get to call family. One a college counselor. Some are from my Bay Area roots. A few were influential while I attended college in San Diego. Some will never know that I see them as a mentor. Anne Lamott falls into the latter category. I'd often hear a line from one of her books, passed in dialogue between a college roommate and one of my Communication professors. They'd reel over some of her earlier books like *Plan B*, *Bird by Bird* and *Traveling Mercies*, quoting philosophies and paragraphs. These books were stacked caddy-whompus among others in the corner of our La Mesa apartment bedroom. When I hear others rant and rave about almost anything, I hesitate to jump in. It's like the expectation builds before reason or actual want and I fight against that. And that's what happened with every Anne Lamott book I'd hear about during college until my final undergrad semester when I unpreparedly hit the wall. Every time I sat to write or research and list- wall. Every study session- wall. Every test- wall. Presentation- wall. I couldn't move beyond my own resistance to learning. Was it learning? Whatever it was, it was ruthless. And my professor saw it. She saw the doubt and hesitancy in my exams and in my writing samples. She saw the slump in my defeated eyes and noteless papers. She likely saw the symptoms of need long before I recognized them and she took me to lunch on a Friday- a day she didn't have to teach. A day she could have introverted in her office grading or preparing for the following week. A day she could have been home with her family. She could have spent that time running errands or the world, but she stepped in to my setback.

There was a small Whole Foods-type market neighboring the East County San Diego Starbucks many of us would regular before an anticipated final or date. We grabbed pre-packaged salads and a box of crackers, two sparkly waters and an outdoor table on the concrete patio. I was sure we'd talk mostly about my grades and the latest Ethnography paper that I didn't do so well on, but instead she got straight to the nitty questions about my latest heart break, missing my Bay Area-based family, and the unfortunate, obnoxious roommate dynamics. Relationships give me life and she knew that well. She knew that I was stretched in the unbalance of loss and love and she didn't have to know my whole story to know that I was not okay. She knew that my wall was not academic but emotional. Lamott's *Bird by Bird* was referenced about five million times, quite possibly it was only two or three, but for the gross imagination it was five million and each time with the intention to encourage and restore movement. I'd wrestle against her and this book in my own passive way by diverting from the obvious truth having not even read it, but she'd steady the course, leading me back to focus. Leading with the roots. Leading me like good teachers do so well. She gently offered her own stories of loss or grief, each with a dose of humor and connection and I was grateful for all of them.

    For weeks I had prayed to move beyond the barriers of that wall, assuming it was other-based. It's more comforting to the human condition when the problem is external. *I'm not unwell; you're unwell.* Leaving our lunchtime conversation, I realized it was my own stubbornness molding the barriers around and within me. I held tightly to assumptions, lies, preferences and insecurities that gave structure to my broken frame.

    Before the days of Amazon Prime you had to drive to a bookstore, so I went to the closest Barnes and Noble in San Diego County and made myself a promise. This book was an investment. I was living on a church intern salary and the $16.00 book was not in my initial budget, but then again, neither were those Rainbow sandals I bought the weekend prior. I was giving myself the gift of grit and growth. This professor believed in me. She believed in my writing and in my stories, lived and yet lived. She saw my character and my purpose. She challenged my perspective on self-potential. *Bird by Bird* was, indeed, an investment. A great investment. The maddening wall wasn't permanent like I had built it up to be and it came down, brick by brick, exposing cracked and rotting roots, just like the professor alluded to. I didn't like my story so far, but Anne convinced me, in my brain of brains, that there lives the possibility for vindicated potential. It was as clear as day, the freedom to release myself, or at least to begin to release myself into my own story. Anne says, *You own everything that happened to you. Tell your stories. If people wanted you to write warmly about them, they should have behaved better (Bird by Bird).* Beyond abuse. Beyond disaster and loss and break-ups. Beyond brokenness, I get to tell tell my story. Because it's mine and I'm guessing somewhere in all of this, it might be yours too.

It's now been almost twelve years since first reading Lamott's *Bird by Bird*, mostly read sitting with my extra hot Chai tea latte like every other white girl in San Diego, along a Barnes and Noble end-cap that day. I'm still the teachable mentee of the unaware Anne. She accompanies me on most vacations, packed tightly into a carry on duffle, joining me for morning coffee. Maybe even sitting in the hot tub with me and Tempranillo. Like good mentors, she's there. Unaware of it, but there.

    A few years ago, Eric and I rented a small cabin that was built around an old water tower along the Mendocino coast. Early the first morning, as Eric was still asleep, I crept out of the bedroom and into the living room, nestled between the base of the tower beams. Anne sat on the faux leather couch, waiting patiently as I first made coffee and then she shared these words:

I was learning the secrets of life: that you could become the woman you'd dared to dream of being, but to do so you were going to have to fall in love with your own crazy, ruined self (Small Victories: Spotting Improbable Moments of Grace).

    I had glimpses of what it could look like to be who I wanted to be. The daring eleventh grader who stood up to her teacher with lawyer-sized notes. To be the buckled preteen who stared down her abuser because enough was enough. But even though there were glimpses of strength, my greater belief system told me these markings were fixed in weakness and wreckage.

    We operate from our truth systems- from the beliefs we've accumulated in life through experience or word. Whether they are assumed or concluded, even if they are flawed with lies and trip-ups, if we believe these ideas and resolves, they grow roots and we water their function with likewise cases. These ideas tell us who we are, what we deserve and what we don't. They convince us of another's intentions or abilities. They dictate progress and set backs. My belief system, though having known about God since I breathed on my own, told me I was too broken for His love. My identity was muted by the cracks in purity, wholeness and courage. Those ideals had fallen and been crushed by the weight of what had happened to me. I wanted to love my crazy, ruined self, but I wasn't ready. It was all too much. I was too much. I didn't believe that I, in my story, could really make a mark on someone because I was already marked by the acts of another.

CHAPTER TWO: COFFEE AND CRUMB DUST

It took six years, thousands of dollars, seven moves, three schools and a partridge in a pear tree but I graduated from college. I'm positive my parents were just as relieved as I was to finally be done and off their payroll. I graduated with my Bachelors degree just weeks before my twenty-fourth birthday. Two days later, I packed my Toyota Tacoma like the greatest Tetris game I'd ever play, saving just enough room in the passenger seat for Starbucks and the Spirit, and began the long drive north to San Jose. Opportunities for work and further education led me home. For the three years I lived in San Diego, I drove this four hundred and fifty or so miles six or more times. Each time before, I'd take the 5 freeway. I had no patience for road work and slow coastal drivers along Highway 1 on a Friday or holiday weekend. This time I planned for savor. I put my toes in the sand somewhere near Huntington Beach. I stopped at a thrift store in Malibu. Grabbed food as I passed through Santa Barbara. Spent an appropriate amount of time strolling through Pismo, nostalgically driving up to where I spent most summers and holidays with my Nana at what was her home on a hill with a view. I thought about that summer after high school graduation when I got my first tattoo, a tramp stamp before I knew any better, at a corner parlor about two blocks from the beach I was now sitting on. I laughed about how disappointed it made all of my grandparents.

    I drove all day. I let myself feel both the exhaustion and release of school. I let myself miss friends and an old boyfriend. I let myself cry sobbing and hideous tears and sing every country radio song wrong. I let myself grieve the idea of moving back in with my folks. And I let myself scroll through embarrassing and impacting relationships, conversations and experiences like movie scenes in my head. Frame by frame. Like in high school, when I jabbed a number two pencil into my thigh during Algebra 2 to get the attention of the new cute boy who happened to sit next to me. Neither of us knew what the teacher was instructing and this seemed like the right move. I've been wrong before. He was more concerned than attracted, as any sane person would have been. I thought about the next year when eight of us friends, including the concerned pencil to thigh observer, crammed ourselves into a caterpillar limo for the senior dance. I thought about how lucky I had it to work with high school students for those years during college, and what a gift it was to lead them overseas each summer and witness their connection to global ideas of faith. I thought about my long-term high school boyfriend and how ridiculously nervous I was during those first few landline phone calls, hoping my brother wouldn't pick up somewhere else in the house and listen in. I thought about when he asked me on my first real date. My mom took me shopping at Express for a coordinating skirt and cardigan because it was 1999 and we were both convinced this is what a first date needed, coordinates. That boy picked me up and we went to Golfland. He was showing off his swing, and accidentally hit my thumb with the metal putter. I wanted to sob with the pain and embarrassment, but high school love is a real thing and he could do no wrong, so I was fine.

My mind went loop dee loop with my third Starbucks White Chocolate Mocha. Over, under and through nearly every stand-out memory during what turned in to an almost fifteen hour trek back home.

I missed the friends I left in San Diego. I looked forward to reconnecting with friends in the Bay Area. I wondered if anyone missed me. I thought about the ride or dies. The honest kinds. The no-make-up, thrown together watching the Bachelor and eating waffles connections. The soul bursting, life breathing conversations. Like my dreamy friendship with Jen Hatmaker that she doesn't yet know exists. The friendships that are tested and credible.

Do you ever wonder why there are stories from your life that just won't quit? They come back yearly, sometimes weekly. About a year after high school graduation, I met a girl friend at one of our favorite and local coffee shops. Once we got our driver's licenses, we'd frequent the downtown with our super rad Abercrombie polo shirts and puka shell necklaces like it was our full-time jobs. We've shared dinner tables and dance floors, embarrassing fears and break-ups. We lip sync'd and powder puffed together. We've shared vacations and adventures. We've sang our hearts out to boy bands and Britney. There was so much life lived between us and this day was just an addition to the promise of years ahead. Sitting down together felt like a normal afternoon. Like the distance of months and miles between us were non-existent.

There was nothing physically different about her. Her hugs just as warm and tight. Her ambitions just as notably high. Her temperament just as sweet. We ordered two Chocolate Coffee Creams and two giant ginger cookies. She snagged the end of a six person table along the cracked brick wall and the flood of teenage excitement commenced as we took over each of those seats with our purses and stories. About an hour into recounting classes and teachers and boyfriends, she paused. It was the long blink that got me. The take-in-a-deep-breath-and-fasten-your-eyes-shut kind of blink. It seemed like minutes before she opened them, but then suddenly there she was, staring at the table and then back to me. For the first time I saw her nervous. And then I was nervous. She fiddled with the napkin and then with her straw, unsure of how to tell me and I was sure she was going to tell me something. Her words were mainly a backstory of *this guy* and how they *did things* and how *weird it all was*. I was no innocent apple at this point, carrying my own baggage to the coffee shop that day, and while she shimmied around the main event, I mentally rationed scenarios and moved ginger crumb dust between my fingers and the table top. Then she said the words. Everything I had guessed was wrong.

It was the A word. A big A word. A word I never thought would be used in my inner circle to describe something one of my friends did. Not because we were better than but because I had it in my head that faith would steer us differently.

There were a lot of other A words I would have rather heard that day.

Adorable.
Anesthesia.
Antelope.
Apples.
Amanda.
Antarctica.
Arbor.
Anything.

But never, in any thought leading up to seeing her, did I think Abortion would be what we talked about. And hers. Her abortion. This word was now equated there, with her and in our favorite coffee shop, and I didn't know how to take it in. For the first time in our friendship, I didn't know how to respond to her.

I used to and still sometimes have the awful habit of silence. During uncomfortable situations or times of grief, I'd resort to saying nothing. If I couldn't agree with myself on what the perfect response would be, I'd just sit or stand paralyzed with the fear of perception. It wasn't an intentional response of silence, more like a knee jerk non-response, but I now find myself too vigorous, asking too many questions and engaging a little too much. Sometimes with strangers. Whatever, one day I'll find balance. Maybe.

Our conversations after that day became less frequent and more hostile. She didn't feel like she could trust me with the information, though I was sworn to secrecy and I held it. In all honesty, I was afraid to even mutter those words outside of our table of ginger crumbs and coffee remnants. There was a deep part of me that didn't believe it was true. I didn't want it to be true for her. I didn't want her to know that kind of pain or uncertainty. I didn't want shame developed in her life. We didn't know how to share life after that, and if I'm being honest, I didn't know how to love her. I loved her to the core, I just didn't know how to be a support in the uncharted seas of the great A. For years and years, it ate me up inside to think of her going through that mostly alone. I had so many questions but didn't know how to ask them so I resorted to the distance between us. The last thing I hoped to do was offend her, but with my silence and uneasiness to engage in this wild unknown, that's exactly what I did.

CHAPTER THREE: CROWNS OF CONTROL

I went to high school with a beauty queen. Like, an actual ribboned pageant contestant. Her thin, six foot frame was incredibly intimidating but she didn't judge our differences and we became great friends within the first few months of our freshmen year. Midway through sophomore year, my family moved across town. Conveniently for our friendship, and my parent's sanity, her family lived just up the street from our new house. I swear, I spent more days and nights there than in my own home. We'd jump and lay on the trampoline, looking at the sky and talking about our crushes and classes, the latest dance, and dreaming up what the rest of that year would look like. We talked about the pressures we each faced in different ways and had no idea what any of it really meant.

I mentioned before that I'm now a questioner. My sister says it more like I get people talking and she often relies on that when other family members are around. But it's true- I question a lot. I try not to make people feel intimidated but I'm just so curious about what makes your world go round.

    I was not as eloquent with my questioning in high school. One of our trampoline days, she mentioned this, that and the other about pageantry and fearing her waist size. I couldn't hold back and swirled around my words, which led to, *but you're so skinny so what does it matter?* Though it targeted my wonderment because she had to have been somewhere in the 0-2 size range and I just could not bypass that fact, my chins all came out as I got fifteen year old swirly and spun it right 'round. Like a record baby.

    Food is the one thing I can control because I need to look this way, she told me. And I've yet to forget that. An immediate response held by her belief. Maybe along the way some fool told her she needed to be a certain weight or waist size in order to compete in pageants. Maybe someone else told her she had to tighten it up to win. Maybe someone convinced her that food is in fact the enemy. Maybe her self-value was held up by the crown. And misbelief upon insecurity built up a web of controlled togetherness. But was anyone affirming how wonderful she already was? Was anyone telling her that she had a choice? Was anyone celebrating the fuel of food and how our bodies need it? Would she have listened? At that time, I had ended my career as a non-good, non-professional gymnast and cheerleader, and had transitioned to the swimming and diving teams at our high school. I couldn't think of not eating and I tried, as unfortunately many teenage girls do, but I would've passed out in the 50 free sprint. One hundred thousand percent I wouldn't have made it across the pool. In all of the ways I was jealous of her beauty, jealous of the amount of boys who swooned for her, and jealous of the spotlight that so effortlessly seemed to follow her, I felt sad that day but I also understood. At fifteen, struggling with my own identity, I wanted to scream her value from the mountain top. I wanted to shake her right off that trampoline. Her crown equated control. The control was necessary for her and a similar kind of control was what kept me mostly intact.

It is both reckless and orderly. Fear-based and freeing. The idea of having control over your body, over your emotions, over a circumstance or another person, is all so real. We can convince ourselves that we are really in control of how we feel and how we react or respond, of how we engage or who we engage with. Over our process. Over our future. Over the outcome.

I thought that when I told him to stop and it stopped, that it was over. I thought those years of panic and pain and hatred would surely be behind me. I had come this far, smoke screening the perspective of my life with fineness, that no one even questioned the darkness they didn't see.

Not only did I believe the lies, but I fed them and rested in their soil. Lies were more assuring of truths because if I let myself believe the truth, the whole truth, then I'd have to admit just how shattered I was. I'd have to admit the years of shame and guilt that extinguished any light left. I'd have to admit who this person was and how it made me feel. I managed years of undetected behavior, manipulating situations, friendships and boyfriends to get the outcome I created in my head. To be in control and not feel vulnerable to pain, life became a way of hiding and replacing. If I was a gymnast, then I wasn't really molested. If I joined the leadership class, then I wasn't really a disaster. If I moved to a Christian camp and attended a Christian college, I didn't have to acknowledge that I was also the girl sleeping around and getting Smirnoff wasted most weekends.

    I wanted a new story. I didn't want to be the broken girl, the messy girl, the experienced girl. I wanted my crown and I was willing to do almost anything to make that secure.

CHAPTER FOUR: DIRT BOX AND DA BIND MIN

When Eric and I bought our first home, there were about 3,412 things that needed replacing, fixing, and removing. There was a blood red wall that ran the length of the living and dining room. Joanna would have barfed. The yards, both front and back, each had their own long lists of to-do's, to-cut's, to-move's, and to-redo's. If you opened the sliding door from the dining room into the backyard, you'd play your bet as you walked onto make-shift, half termite-eaten wood steps that the previous owner attempted, leading down to a partially put together uncovered brick patio. We were like most young married couples, broke as the day is long, and our time was spent between multiple jobs and, because Eric was at that time a youth pastor, church responsibilities. By the time our first child, Izzy, was born, we'd done some mostly esthetic changes to the house and yards. Bye bye blood wall. Another one of those changes was taking up some of the broken bricks and disposing of the plastic sheets that had been laid down over a damp mixture of dirt and sand. As Izzy grew, it became one of her favorite places to play because what is life when you spend hundreds of dollars on Montessori-type Melissa and Doug toys, just to see your kid choosing the dirt-sand box? It sat just on the outside of the kitchen window, so after our second daughter was born, I could wash dishes and monitor both kids from where I stood.

    Post-church one Sunday, I was making lunch while Izzy played with what became sand toys in the dirt box. She had been rambling in almost two year old talk all the way home about a *bind min*. She wasn't asking us questions, but had mumbled toddler jargon for almost 10 minutes between the church parking lot and our garage. So as most attentive parents do, Eric and I just listened and responded, *Yeh sis. Cool.*

Our middle, Abigail, was tucked into her swaddle cocoon next to the couch. Lunch was almost ready and rest was coming. Then Izzy screamed. The kind of penetrating scream that makes glass and your heart shatter. I couldn't run fast enough out of the slider and down the broken steps. Her face was covered in wet, dirty sand. *How was it this wet for such a sunny day? It didn't rain. We didn't have sprinklers.* Nothing was making sense.

I carried her inside, cleaning as much sand from the dirt box off of her sweet little freckled face. *Sister, what happened?*

Jes hills da bind min.
Jes hills da bind min.

All I could do was offer sweet loves, her water bottle, and the well-adored grey Jellycat Ellie. Ellie fixes a multitude of tears. After all of the mess was off of her face and safely out from her eyes, she sat down to eat her sandwich as I unpacked her backpack and both of our emotions. There was a check-in paper letting me know that a diaper had been changed, a snack was eaten, and songs were sung. I pulled out a few coloring pages with applesauce pouch remnants smeared over the backs and one soft yellow fold out pamphlet detailing the teaching lesson in the Infant and Toddler room. I'll give you one guess as to which Bible reference they taught. Oh sweet baby Jesus. Izzy had been spitting onto the dirt-sand, making mud like Jesus did when he healed the blind man. It all made sense.

In the last year, from leadership down, ideas and processes are being challenged in and amongst our local church body. (Side note: I fully believe this needs to happen everywhere, in every church and organization and family. Amen.) But it hasn't been handled with much unity and unfortunately sides have been forged. Though Eric and I didn't choose a side because this isn't high school, it seemed like a side had been chosen for us. Months have passed and the tension is, unfortunately, still evident in our community and, lamentably in some of our friendships. In my own insulated nest of thoughts and judgement, wrestling with ideas and conclusions that were obviously right and trying to balance silence and engagement, I didn't realize that I could've been wrong. A dear friend was feeling like an outcast and disrespected and what I thought were my safe boundaries around the issue, became distance. I've known this friend for fifteen years. Our friendship dates back to before I married her friend. Before I moved here to this small town. When we were still in our early twenties trying to build confidence in hair styles and we knew we needed to talk this out. From where I stood it looked like pride. In her, not in me of course. In my prayers to see what God wanted exposed, I put my agenda and unfortunately but truthfully, my judgement aside. There was information we had both heard. Things I knew and wanted her to know and things she knew and wanted me to know. But none of that was as necessary as hearing why she was hurting and working towards finding common ground. This morning we met downtown for Farmers Market coffee and the walk we've done a hundred times before in the early morning hours before work places and babies awoke. Side streets led our conversation and brought us to the high school track where we walked and talked and walked some more.

I still felt right at mile marker one. The ideas and perceptions I had were valid and the case I had built for why I was right was gaining momentum. And then she made a comment and the pillar I stood on, that I was convinced was a concrete rock, was in fact sand. I had been judging her positioning in this all wrong. I stood by my assumptions rather than hearing her truth. I didn't consider her story.

My own quiet conclusions without engaging in and trusting our friendship made me blind. I think there's wisdom in taking a step back to process and certainly not engaging in gossip, but it was my pride not hers and my unwillingness to offer support despite differences that created space for judgement. And the thing is, who am I to judge? I completely respect this person. It's very obvious that we disagree on most political and some social levels, but those disagreements don't break our friendship. They strengthen it.

Friends, we have every opportunity to listen to someone, even when we're so sure they are wrong. My mama used to tell me, *You can't be right about everything.* Sure, that was a fed-up mom putting her angsty daughter in place but it is completely accurate. If we don't take the time to engage in with another's *why*, we may never learn just how wrong and blind we are. Maybe you don't want to know and I get that.

It's been a constant prayer through writing this book that God would expose every truth and every discomfort. Every story that needs to be told. Every vulnerable part of me that needs to be shared so that someone like you could read it and feel connected, heard and valued. And let me tell you He has done just that. Rock over rock, boulder over boulder, God has been yanking me up and out by my unpolished toes, sometimes while I clutch to even the smallest pebble keeping me under the covers. It's uncomfortable and messy and humbling, but it's also completely sanctifying.

Had I stayed under the stones of rightness, I would have lost that friend. I'm sure of it.

Jes hills da bind min.

He certainly does, kid. He certainly does.

CHAPTER FIVE: UP-ROOTED IN UN-FORGIVENESS

If you've learned anything about me so far, it's probably that I'm stubborn, which is likely why I believe God goes the lengths He does to uproot me. In 2007 I was working in youth ministry for a large San Diego-based church. During this time I was attending an adjacent Christian college. Because of that I had tremendous opportunities to hear from phenomenal speakers and writers between weekly chapel and Sunday sermons. It wasn't uncommon to be recommended a book or an author and for as long as I can remember I have loved to read, so I wrote down almost every recommendation anyone offered. I didn't always read them, but you better believe I wrote them down just in case. And then *The Shack*. Unless you were in a coma somewhere between 2007 and 2009, you've likely heard of William P. Young's controversial bestseller. I'd walk through our college coffee shop and there it would be- in the young hands of college students. In the briefcases of professors. We'd be in chapel and the speaker would reference it more than once. This book became a source of dialogue and arguments for more than one of my classes. My roommates were reading it. Family members were reading it. It was everywhere and because it was everywhere I wanted nothing to do with the hype. We've touched on my pride, right?

Casual-like, I'd blow it off like I just wasn't that into fiction genres. I'm not sure if people didn't buy it (there's a reason I'm not an actress), or if God convinced everyone I needed to read it, but I blinked and had 10 copies. An aunt living in the Seattle area sent me one with a note and short article about the author. A prior housemate left one on my windshield. One was given to me as a Christmas present. But I couldn't do it. I didn't open any of the copies. I couldn't muster it up to read even a few words of the first chapter. So I started giving them away. As I'd hand one out, another one would come in. A rotating pendulum of annoyance.

My head logic said I needed to prepare myself for being ruined and I was sure that I would be by this book because that seemed to be every Shack-reader's interpretation of the story. But in reality, we can never fully prepare ourselves for how or when God shatters that rose petal glass we cover our lives with. When all the things, or even just one thing falls apart, we are starkly and keenly aware of just how broken, boiled and needy we are. Stones uprooted again.

Over and over I'd cry out, *Where are you, God?* For years, I'd lament over the loneliness I felt at ten. And at eleven. And year after year my cries settled into fumes of anger. He didn't rescue me. If God wouldn't control this, I would. I'd control how I felt, what I did and who I'd let in.

It was my second year at this Christian college and I was unknowingly desperate for change. Up to that point, all of my relationships were leveled by insecurity. Only an infant's handful of people knew about the sexual abuse and it made me all kinds of uncomfortable just knowing they knew, but I had stayed mostly silent about it for fear of greater shame. For fear that all of what that person told me would turn out to be true. That it was, in fact, my fault.

    Our college had a covered, outdoor coffee bar on campus and most of us between or before class would find our way to a table with laptops and flirty smiles. I'm not even sure now what time of year it was, so we'll go with the middle. I do remember it was cold, but Southern California cold, so can I actually call it *cold*? So in the cold-ish, middle of the year, as I wildly typed a paper that was due fifteen minutes later, the school counselor pulled out a chair to join me. We had only one interaction prior to this and that was through a mutual friend. I couldn't remember this counselor's first name but admired her Anthropologie-esque style. There was no way I was going to finish this paper so I let myself engage. Within a few minutes she was telling me that the Lord had put me on her heart, and a few minutes after that we had scheduled a time to meet.

Every day until that meeting I wanted to cancel. I almost did. I'd walk by her office, hoping to leave an ambiguous note that *something came up*, but she was always there and I didn't have the galls (with a capital B) to admit my lack of commitment, hence the English paper I never finished from that day she first sat down with me.

So I showed up and to my surprise I wasn't the only one. She had invited two other female students. After introducing myself to them, I learned that the two of them were already friends. The counselor gave each of us a white sheet of printer paper and set markers, crayons and pencils on her desk as though waiting for a group of Kindergarteners to walk in and join the counseling soiree. She asked us to draw a picture from our childhood. Picture instead the head turn and hear the voice of my favorite comedian, Anjelah Johnson, as I flipped my saucy brown hair away from my shoulders, *Excuse me, no.* They just learned my name and now I'm going to share about my childhood with these student strangers in some weird child therapy discourse? Was I getting college credits for this? I sat in my head while the other two began to draw. Softies. While they drew and I glared, the counselor began talking. And then I began listening. It was her story and it sounded a lot like mine. I grabbed a pencil and drew one person, and then another, and then another. I added the sun and also darkness by way of black clouds. I added a Bible and a flower and something red. I cried as we listened to her story and I wondered *why us*. Why was she so vulnerable with us? Did she invite more students but they were successful with their fleeting notes, and now only the three of us dared to show? When she said God put me on her heart, why did He do that?

One by one we were invited to share our story. As much or as little as we felt comfortable to share. I was the last to go and I could have summed it all up with *same*. Sexual abuse and molestation were a part of all of our stories. Living behind lies of control and fear, shame and insecurity, we were all connected to trauma, but we were all also, in this sacred moment, connected to mercy. Connected to the fight for light- to finally be seen and free. Experiencing empathy for each of those women that evening gave me hope for that in return.

The months following our initial Color and Counsel (way less fun than a Brush and Cork- at least there's alcohol there), we'd casually meet when we could, championing one another towards healing by way of encouraging notes or coffee. This counselor, who became a dear mentor, encouraged me to finally open up to my family and tell the whole truth. One of the lies I believed, a captive lie from my abuser was that my family wouldn't believe me. But this counselor, stepping in to show me her belief, helped me to see that this pillar of fear was in fact faulty sand. She believed me. The other girls believed me. I believed myself and that became enough to secure my stance in the fight. I was done being silent about it. I booked my Southwest flight home for one weekend. Before I boarded my flight, I called my parents and told them that we needed to talk. No one wants a talking to. The ideas I'm sure they thought and talked through before my arrival must've been wild. Had I quit college in hopes of getting cast for the Bachelor? Was I changing majors or colleges again? They didn't see it coming and I almost felt bad for ruining their weekend. They could have gone about gardening and living in the empty-nestedness, but now they were parents to a girl who had been molested.

    The lies convinced me they wouldn't believe me. He told me they'd shame me and I'd be blamed. Something in me feared that their love wouldn't be great enough once they knew. And then they heard every word I said. They collected their thoughts and hugged me tight and we all fell apart, and every single lie between us burst into flames.

In the months following, my dad began asking me what forgiveness looked like. Not in the basic query, but in the very personal, *Have you and do you think you can ever forgive this person?* It wasn't a forcing question with opposition or motive, but rather the build up to a faith steering conversation. Up to this point, I had never even considered forgiving him. Yeh right, man. I hated him. Hate even seemed like too kind of a word. But my dad, in a way that only he can do with his Bono-like features and calming kindness, asked those questions and they stuck, sharp in my side, shooting at me like labor pains without the hope of birth. I couldn't do it yet and no one was forcing me to. I wasn't ready to let go of the fury, the injustice.

I finally read *The Shack*, finishing most of it in a pile of tears on the bathroom floor, but that'll come in another chapter. If you're familiar with Young's book, you know how the father's story of grief evolves and where it settles. If you've yet to read it because you were in that coma, or you're hard-headed like myself (solidarity), here's the short: It settles in forgiveness. Forgiving himself and forgiving the person who took his daughter. It's wild and messy, his road to the shack. He's saturated with anger, disbelief and agony over what should never have been. The father eventually meets a three-fold collective, symbolizing the Trinity- God the Father, Son and Holy Spirit. These characters, each with their purpose and knowledge in who this man is, lead him in a series of questions, experiences and visions. None of this offers leisure or ease, but all of it necessary to release him from the captivity of unforgiveness. Isn't that the truth?

If I couldn't yet forgive him, could I at least forgive myself? Could I begin to forgive God for not stepping in? Could I trust that God was in the business of restoring my faith in Him, in myself and in the system of justice? Could I trust that the One who holds forgiveness, does so with blood in His hands?

CHAPTER SIX: MIND THE TRAFFICK(ING)

For the good love, Christians breathe the air of conferences. During the three years I lived in San Diego, my time must have aligned with the Age of them. It seemed like every other month, our youth staff was either attending a conference, planning one or hearing about another.

One took us up to Los Angeles- a place where traffic is only justified for the Ellen Show or Celebrity Rap Superstar (holler at me, Run DMC). I wasn't thrilled for another conference and guesstimated, while sitting packed between the other four million cars trudging through the 405 freeway, just how many of these youth workers would rededicate their lives to Jesus during one of the seventeen alter calls throughout this three-day event. After unloading our bags and my judgement into hotel rooms, we shuffled ourselves into the convention center and into our seats. The conference opened with a singer-songwriter introducing herself and then a short video that played on the large screens behind her. It first looked like an overseas mission proposal, something to be expected here, but then the narrator kept saying things like *human trafficking and modern day slavery,* and I became assertively aware of what I didn't know. Once the video was over, singer Kendall Payne shared of learning about human trafficking which inspired her song *Touch*. The words were so powerful and I could hardly contain the nauseating questions mixed with trying-to-hide emotions covering my face.

    I can't tell you who the keynote speaker was or which peripheral topics we covered in break-out sessions. I can't even tell you the name of this particular conference but I can tell you that God stopped me there. My pride of a know-it-all Christian was standing in the way of learning what He had for me. As soon as the session from that evening was over, two of us hurried downstairs to meet Kendall in the expo center. I had thousands of questions but could only mutter one, *What do we do about this?*

When I returned home from that weekend, I researched as much as I could, but got lost in FBI sites mostly leading to prostitution. I had flown up to San Jose shortly thereafter, as my first niece was born. After extending my stay for far too long, because hello, I was Auntie Em for the very first time and my heart could both explode and implode simultaneously at the joy of kissing those cheeks, I finally booked my flight back to San Diego. I sat at the terminal, squinting through pictures on my pink flip phone, struggling already to leave my baby niece. I looked up, being pulled back into where I was, as the parents of an old high school friend said my name. Turned out they were on the same flight, visiting their son who was also living in the area. Their presence gave me necessary comfort and distraction, plus the known company on any flight was more than welcomed so we continued our conversation from the terminal to the plane. I had still been reeling over learning about human trafficking just weeks prior, so when my friend's mom asked, *What else is new?*, I couldn't help but dive in and let it all pour out. She nodded along as I rambled and then mentioned that her son had also been telling her similar stories. One of his professors had taught on issues of injustice, highlighting trafficking and his involvement in prevention and education. My friend's mom encouraged me to call her son and get the contact for his professor. No sooner did I get off the plane did I call him, and by the following week I had an appointment to meet this professor at his Point Loma law office.

No one, at that point in my life, would describe me as a punctual person. I was still living in the fashionably late dream of yesteryear. Now I'm a mom and I'll never have that luxury again. But for this anticipated meeting I was early. I walked in and was greeted by his office assistant, who let me know that Mr. Goff would be there shortly.

Side note: I knew that this story would make its way into the book, but I had to prepare myself for it. Not because it's an unworthy or pointless one but because I feared being perceived as that person. You know that person. The one who drops names and associations like it's what their whole life is about- who they know. My friends, I am a lot of things but being that person is for sure not one of them. When we met he was not the fame-known Bob Goff he is today. It's completely weird to reference him but in the same breath, meeting Bob was an intricate part of my back story. I wouldn't feel right about leaving that out simply because of a possible eye roll from someone reading this, thinking I'm that person. End side note.

I took a seat and noticed how sweaty my elbow creases were. I had thousands of questions, but again only one came out when we finally took our seats in his office, *How do you know about this?* During those next few hours he pulled out books and pictures and stories. All first hand. I was shocked and amazed, horrified and hopeful. His words were full of action. He gave me a book that he wrote and then encouraged me to buy a few others to round out the story of trafficking. He shared with me about what it was like to pull people out of these situations, providing safety and dignity. Though he didn't know any of my story, his words of compassion and response cut right to the sticky mess of my own heart and the questions that reeled over why I felt unsaved. Not in the faith-sense of the term, but in the very true wondering why so many, including myself, aren't pulled into immediate safety from harmful situations.

    I left his office that afternoon with a promise that he'd speak to our youth group, and a handful of organizations to contact. Aimlessly with a spinning mind around trafficking, I drove down the coastline, settling into every word, story and feeling. Every word of crime. Every story of rescue. Every feeling of un-resolve. Each challenge the law firm faced in the States and overseas when it came to generating and upholding policies. Every emotion that begged *this is wrong so how can it be?* My heart hurt for those people. Hurt doesn't even feel like the right word to use here. It's too shallow. Too flippant. I remember asking God how this happens. How so many are held captive and why this isn't more newsworthy than a celebrity's botched hair cut or new pilates routine. Why are so many gaining from the wreckage of lives? How didn't I know about this before Kendall's song? Why was the research so limited? It's such a broad evil and as I drove along North Harbor and the waterfront, and through the city and back to my East County apartment, God called me into forgiveness, not understanding. I thought meeting Bob would give me clarity about issues of trafficking and it did, but what God had for me that day was more. That day He exposed my un-forgiveness over the person who molested me and showed me how I was using one more thing, and a good thing at that, to distract me from the inevitable- facing the pain that was robbing me from wholeness. I was learning that harboring seeds of forgiveness would only deepen the roots of pain.

Fast forward three years when a dear friend and I joined a Bay Area-based NGO team to research and observe just a glimpse into human trafficking through Cambodia and Thailand. My research thus far had led me to hundreds of conversations, volunteering hours with the Not For Sale Campaign, speaking to churches and high school groups, and the opportunity to create a local collective to further educate our small, rural community. But I knew there was more I didn't know. More I needed to see. I'm that kind of person, unfortunately or not, who learns holistically. It's not enough for me just to hear it or read it. It needs to be tangible. We spent two weeks at compounds, safe-schools and even a circus, meeting with medical and transit officials, because the effects of human despair spread everywhere. We visited a hospital and learned more about the direct affect that war and poverty has had over these countries and this generation, which has made them vulnerable to human predators. We saw large-scale American clothing factories behind too-tall mortar walls, guarded by men with guns. We sat with rescued women as they crafted toys, baskets and jewelry, while sharing their own stories and desperately wanting more for their children than what they had to endure. The symptoms in those communities led to the awful things of abuse and greed and unlawful gain. The bottom line of evil is so unapologetically unruly.

There was so much to process leaving those places and the people, the contrast of devastation and beauty. The roar of the quiet. On the plane I re-read journal entries from those two weeks and emails I sent to my family from small wicker chairs in tea cafe's. I looked through videos and photographs. I stared into their eyes and joined their smiles, wondering how much gumption it took just to do that- smile. I wondered how the greatest of this injustice would ever find resolve. And just like that, I was back driving around San Diego in my Toyota Tacoma, settling in to the unsettledness of it all. Between sleep and on-board movies, between cups of water and airplane coffee, again and again I found God echoing forgiveness over understanding. For who, other than God Himself, can fully understand the ways of the wicked? Who, other than God alone, has the Sovereign power to bear witness to the gravity of sin? And who, more than any other, understands the greatness of our transgressions and forgives us still when we ask?

    I hate injustice. I hate the evil that lurks in our communities and in our own hearts. I hate that it exists. Forgiveness sometimes feels like the easy way out. The cop-out. A way to ignore or deny these heavy-hitting stamps of iniquity. I'm often left questioning, if I forgive this person and move on, how can it be that I also stand firm for justice and righteousness? They haven't seemed to co-exist before. I felt like if I forgave the person who held me captive to shame and fear and abuse, he would just continue the pattern in another way with another person. The act of forgiving him worried me because I couldn't control the follow up to that forgiveness. I couldn't ensure that he wouldn't do this again. But I was also keenly aware that forgiving another person, even when they haven't asked for it, doesn't necessarily mean they are released from fault, but rather that you are released from the chains that connect and keep you there with them.

    I wasn't sure I could trust the holder of that forgiveness until God reminded me that He is the holder and the keeper of forgiveness. I was giving my molester the power he didn't deserve. More than God's abiding in the ways of forgiveness, the Bible tells me that nothing happens without His consent. Join me in Lamentations, a book of grieving towards the later middle collective in the Old Testament.

Nobody can speak and have it happen unless the Lord commands it. Both bad and

good things come by the command of the Most High God.
Lamentations 3:37-38

Maybe, like me, that gives you comfort. Maybe you just read that and you've cinched the three hundredth notch on your belt of anger as you despise any form of a god. Maybe you have questioned everything that's happened in your life and you continue to question why God would allow those things. Why He's allowed cancer and pain. Why He allowed that divorce. Why he's allowed treacherous hurricanes and mass shootings. For me, to know that God has known it all and that nothing that happens to me goes without His foreknowledge changed everything. I needed to know He saw me. I needed to know there was purpose in it and when I consider that God breathes His purpose into everything, I clung there, hanging tightly to what His purpose could look like in my mess.

When I was young, maybe early elementary days, my family attended a small

Lutheran church on the East Side of San Jose. It's where my grandparents went and where my parents began taking my brother and me. The other families there were like families of our own, including the pastor. I'm not sure what it was for now, but at one point, this pastor gave me a small, creamy white Bible with the inscription of Romans 8:28 on the inside front cover. I was confirmed in this Lutheran church at the end of my eighth grade year and given a Max Lucado book from the youth pastor, also with Romans 8:28 on the inside cover. Two years later when I sat in my high school Leadership class, we were asked to share a life verse aloud with the class. I didn't know what that meant, but I knew that at two different points, Romans 8:28 had been shared with me, so I opened my Bible, searched and found the text to claim it in some mild way before my peers.

And we know that in all things God works for the good of those who love him, who are called according to his purpose.

Romans 8:28

That day in Leadership, I read the text and am sure I made up some reason as to why it mattered, but I had no idea how much I would come to revisit Romans. I had no idea then that, just like meeting Bob, my backstory would be incomplete without knowing Romans 8:28, and why I would so desperately fasten to the promise of *all things*.

SECTION TWO:
UNCOVERING ABORTION

CHAPTER SEVEN: SOFTNESS AND ILLUMINATION

You know I'm stubborn and that goes for most things, books included, which is certainly odd since I love to read. Maybe it's just specific. Yes, I'm specific; not stubborn. Wink. It's not all books but mainly hyped faith-based ones. Books about purity, forget it. Books that tell you how to be a perfectly coiffed mom, toss that sucker out with yesterday's gluten. But give me your divorce stories, your heartache and loss, the lessons you've learned from grievous mishaps. Something with a cuss word, sure. Give me the real. That's my butter.

Recently I read a stint of fiction books, some historical, some romantic-like, some business. Until last year, the amount of non-academic fiction books I had read in my lifetime could have been counted on one hand. On two fingers. I voluntarily read two fiction books until a sweet writer friend of mine swirled me in to what she was writing and who her influencers are and I agreed to read whatever books she'd let me borrow. I had led with the belief that if it wasn't real, it didn't matter. I was sure there was nothing I could learn from fiction books, but as you've seen, I've been wrong before. And I was certainly wrong again.

I started with Rachel Hollis' fiction series from *Party Girl* to *Sweet Girl* and *Smart Girl*. Which led to *One Day in December* by Josie Silver and then I was hooked. With all of the crazy in our own lives, it's anchoring to live in fantasy for a moment. It's fascinating the way words can both convey and create a world of belief. Though I love me some good romantic fiction with my glass of wine, my bread is still non-fiction. I will butter it up with solidarity.

When Lysa TerKeurst announced her newest book, *It's Not Supposed To Be This Way,* her title was clever and relevant and I knew I needed to read her words. I had somewhat loosely been following along with her social media posts and knew this book was breathed from debris she didn't warrant, which is unashamedly and most definitely why I was drawn to it. The clutter in marriage and health and her tendencies to resolve what had been, paralleled some of my current thoughts and motives. Immediately I found comfort there with her, like sitting on the porch with sweet tea and tears as we shared how God has gone before us in what seems like a disaster, only to draw us deeper there with Him.

Do you see it, Em?

Sometimes it's like it was yesterday, but I remember laying in my bed that night. It was just weeks after my twenty-fourth birthday.

What would I say to my parents?
How would I tell them?
I'll have to quit my summer job as a camp counselor.
This is humiliating.

I remember Google-ing what a miscarriage felt like and looked like to get the details right. I remember knowing what my lie would be and how to spin it. The cramps and blood were real. The pain was real. The emptiness was real. The tears. Oh the tears. But the reason I wasn't pregnant anymore was a lie. How was I going to admit it to anyone when I, myself, could hardly stand to believe what I had done.

I had dinner plans near downtown San Diego with friends for my twenty-fourth birthday. I had flown back down just for the weekend and was staying with one of my girl friends. My plane landed early Friday afternoon and since we had some time to do important things, like wander around Target, that's obviously what we did. The weeks and even months prior were full of final papers and exams, presentations and packing. I was exhausted. It felt like a different level of exhaustion, one that also curated random nausea but I chalked it all up to the emotions of leaving a place and people I loved.

We walked each aisle, even the unnecessary ones because that's what Targettes do best- spend copious amounts of time browsing. My friend made an off-handed comment about period cramps and as I nodded along I realized it had been a while. In fact, as I mentally shifted to a time chart, I couldn't, for the life of me, pinpoint my last period. My eyes did the long blink, the blink I was familiar with from that Los Gatos coffee shop. The blink of disbelief because I knew in that moment. I was pregnant.

    Within the hour, the pee stick confirmed.
    Within 24 hours, two other people knew.
    Within 56 hours, I was in a clinical room at Planned Parenthood confirming the ultra sound.
    Within 70 hours, three more people knew.

On May 29, I sat alone on my bed in my parent's home and convinced myself that I could do this- I could be a single mom. There were journal pages, an angry ex-boyfriend on the phone, and my childhood teddy bear confirming.

On June 6, 2008, I was no longer pregnant. The full shift of change was messy, and as Lysa so perfectly spells it out, *When Satan can isolate us, he can influence us.* I wish I had heard those words then, and chose to fill my space with truth and people, but I didn't. It was lonely and that's how I made it. My tendency to hide is either due to introvert hibernation or knowing that I've done something wrong, like a kid hiding in the corner of their closet with poopy pants.

Unfortunately, it was easy to hide. I'd been hiding for years, training myself to live within the hush of a stinky corner. I worked the Christian circuit- camp, school, church, but my association or employment to those things didn't change the way I viewed myself or even sin, for that matter. And there I was on the most claustrophobic day in June, making the very choice I had told myself I'd never make because I never believed it would happen to me. In all the lightyears, never did I believe I'd be the girl who got pregnant without first being a Mrs. It was like living a real Never Have I Ever game, but then I did. Like most improbable scenarios, I hadn't given abortion much thought. Other than the day in Los Gatos, hearing my friend tell me her truth, it just always seemed like an off-topic. Why would I need or care to discuss it? But you never know which way you'll run or saunter or drag yourself at the crossroads. We like to think we do though.

The hiding only escalated from there. Hiding became lying, digging my own grave of isolation. I hand picked who and where, how and when I'd tell people. For months I lived in this lie of having had a miscarriage because surely then my sins would be forgiven. Having sex and getting pregnant now seemed justified somehow because of the sympathy from others in my loss. I even pitied the girl I was talking about. I felt sad she experienced this, even though I knew my own truth and that it was me and that she made a choice. Even still, to live in the lie was much more comforting to these broken bones.

    About two weeks after the abortion, I made a snap call to leave the Bay Area and move back to San Diego. I couldn't face my family and the people I loved there. I could hardly face myself. The lies were as claustrophobic as that day in June. There was a temporary room available with a friend of a friend and I swooped on it. She knew more about me than I did her, but it was oddly comforting not to do the Basic Introduction. *Hi, I'm Emily, blah dee dee blah*. Within the first week I quickly realized she was in the middle of her own shamble. We were running errands around East County, picking up groceries and moving between small talk, when she told me she was pregnant. No more guesses as to why her extra room was temporary. She left no details to the imagination and it was one of those horrifying situations you would pray on no one. This friend of a friend confirmed her choice to abort the baby and as clear as the big, bright, sunny freaking day, God said, *Daughter, share your story.*

Long blink. That kind of immediate obedience felt foreign but I put my head down and told her everything. From the first time I said *miscarriage* to the way the Planned Parenthood rooms smelled. I told her about the procedure I had at almost 16 weeks and that it is nothing like what's promoted or what you think it will be like. I told her how much I had hated myself and God. I told her about my childhood and that I understood what abuse can do. I apologized for where choices had led her that day and for the loneliness of having to make a decision she never wanted to make. I don't know how she looked at me from her drivers seat but when I opened my eyes, we were both crying and for the first time in a very, very long time, I didn't feel hopeless.

The Unaware Anne says, *Grief ends up giving you the two best gifts: softness and illumination.* My story illuminated the reality of that decision, one I hoped she wouldn't make, not because I didn't want her to have a choice, but because I knew what comes from that choice. There was no judgement over her, but empathy. I wish I could tell you the outcome of that story. I wish I could tell you that her baby is alive and well and in elementary school, or that we've remained friends. I wish I could tell you that from that day on, I only shared the truth in obedience. But I don't and I didn't. I stayed in the lie a little longer. Until I couldn't. My story was shared. Without me. Without my consent or knowledge. Without boundaries or grace. It was wildfire. Uncontrolled and ruthless. And I was mortified. Humiliated times a billion.

God, you told me to share my story so I did. Where are you now?

CHAPTER EIGHT: HOLY BERKELEY, BATMAN

Eric and I had only been dating for a few months when *it* got out. A girl I barely knew was told by someone I didn't tell and she made it her point to make sure Eric knew who he was dating. (Oh boy, I really wanted to use a word here. A bad word aimed at this person. But sometimes we have to choose self-control. Just know, I wanted to.) The weeks that followed *it* getting out were consumed by short long-distance phone calls with Eric on the other end breathing doubt, my mind clustered with worry and waiting to see if he'd stay in this or not. Like I said, it was only a few months, but we had known each other for three years at that point. I knew I wanted to be with him. Meanwhile, between assuring Eric that I was sorry for not being honest with him, I was also assuring my parents I didn't need counseling. They were also told not by me, without my consent. See a theme here? I began attending counseling because since I was living back under my parent's roof, had no option otherwise and they saw something happening in me that I didn't yet want to see. At this time, I was working full time in San Jose while simultaneously plowing through my Masters degree. Busyness was distraction and I welcomed all of it. Anything to keep me from pining over a phone call or having to address the downward spiral post-abortion.

Eric lived a few hours away from me, toward the mountains, but asked if I'd join him for a weekend in Oakland to visit two of his close friends who were now married. I agreed as proof of being fine but regretted it twenty minutes in to our drive when he told me that he shared my story with them in order to gain clarity and perspective with whatever his decision would be. According to him, this caused his two friends to become highly suspect of my character, and I one-hundred percent rolled my eyes. Take your average girl, meeting her boyfriend's friends for the first time and the nerves that come with that.

Then replace your average girl with me and my story. Oh, holy Berkeley, Batman. Where's the booze?

We met at a Mexican fusion open-aired restaurant and immediately Eric left me at the table, alone with the wife while he and the husband grabbed drinks and ordered our food. *Thanks, bud.* My breath and my filter left me so I edged along in small talk, going along mostly with questions like, *"how was the drive?"*. I didn't want to be there. I didn't want to prove myself to people I didn't know. My reputation preceded me, and again, like that day in my history class, I internally argued the unfairness of this meet up, their judgement and even the idea that Eric was teetering. Get me my notebook! It's time to bullet point.

I wasn't even openly talking about the abortion with my closest friends. Not even with my parents. And I certainly hadn't processed it within my own self or let alone with God. And now, though there were no direct or abrasive questions, I felt like everything I said or did or didn't say and didn't do was held accountable to perception, and my conclusion was that Eric would lean hard and fast towards a break up. This time we'd spend with his friends would assure us one way or the other. I had no control over which way he'd fall but leaned into my own security with what I wanted and who I was. Every second spent there, I was sure that what I wanted was to be more than a girl who had an abortion and wondered if anyone would ever see me as anything more. Because in every single way, I was more. I am more.

As he drove me home the next day, it was mostly quiet in the white Subaru until he asked me this: *Are you a Christian?*

I know. I laughed too. Excuse my initial response, but *What the hell, man?*

Eric went on to explain that a friend of his, someone he greatly respected, was convinced that someone of faith would never make this choice. Therefore, according to this friend who shall not be named, I was not a Christian. This friend encouraged Eric to confront me and so he did- in the middle of ten thousand cars also leaving Oakland midday that Sunday. Suddenly it felt like those cars' headlights were eyes and they were all staring expectantly at me, waiting for a sure response and agreement that indeed, no one of faith would ever make that choice. I can't even write that with a straight face, you guys.

It took years for me to forgive the assumption, not because it was asked but because I knew it came from a place of ignorance and sometimes we make a call for someone's faith that we have no part in making. Take the Bachelorette, Hannah B. for instance. You don't even have to be a watcher of the franchise show to know what went down with her and Luke P. over their last meal (or pretend meal because why do they never actually eat? If I'm going to marry someone, I better know if he chews with his mouth open or not.). Conservatives blew that trash up on every outlet, dying on the stake that Hannah B. isn't actually a Christian if she openly had sex. No, no, let's instead hide behind the cross to prove our righteousness. Oh glory, hold me back. May we be reminded that Christ, and Christ alone, is the keeper of the saved. We don't get to make that judgement call.

Over and over, I'd sit through agonizing conversations, being the noticeable outcast in Christian circles, hashing and re-hashing details about my choice, and convincing others of proof of regret or character or you name it, until one day I decided that no one gets to decide that except for me. I kid you not, I walked by a group of girls at our wedding (yes, my own damn wedding) and one of them, not so quietly but for sure passively said I should be thankful Eric married me after what I had done. I half expected protest signs to come out during our first married dance. Clearly they were not my choice of invitees, but please, grab your waffles (because breakfast for dinner is always a great idea) and enjoy some wine on us. Maybe they should be thankful my East San Jose side didn't come out swinging.

Slowly, very slowly, through multiple rounds of counseling, giving up my fear of rejection and then deciding not to give a crap who knows, God moved me from a place of proving myself and my faith, to a settledness of being found by forgiveness. If what I believe about who Jesus is and why He came to live and die on the cross is rooted in a generous and kind forgiveness for our sins, who was anyone else, especially a group of mean girls to convince me otherwise?

This probably isn't the last time I'm going to mention Knox McCoy or his book, *The Wondering Years* because I believe his words and thoughts and conclusions are a powerful testimony for generations to hear. Some of his thoughts of grace are this:

Some Christians see grace as a kind of heavenly Febreze that ensures that our souls smell like cotton candy instead of burnt hair, but I find it more helpful to think of grace as permission. Not permission to pursue sin and live in disobedience, but permission to explore the duration of our failures without being shamed. Sin is definitely poison, but so is shame; and grace exists as the antidote of those poisons so we can focus on the lessons we need to learn from our screwup's. The rigidity and stubbornness that motivates the refusal to acknowledge sin and failure can sometimes be just as damaging as a behavior itself.

Boom. That Knox, man.

Sometimes I think we forget that, don't we? As a Christian, we can so often defend our holiness against another's and completely forget the sin causing that is maniacal pride. We send others into a catapult of shame by extorting their sins while withholding grace and call it accountability. I think the great and powerful Oz of Christian writing, C.S. Lewis says it best in the work of Mere Christianity when he writes:

Pride gets no pleasure out of having something, only of having more of it than the next man ... It is the comparison that makes you proud: the pleasure of being above the rest. Once the element of competition is gone, pride is gone.

We battle tirelessly with the need to be above or greater. The need for more. The need to prove our place, our purpose, our stuff against the rest. Social media is the best obvious outlet and case study for this type of competition. If it weren't for social platforms, would you have made what you did for dinner tonight? Or would you have spent copious amounts of money on those subscription boxes with the hope of being an influencer? Would you still have your kids hold those chalkboard Back to School signs? Would you be just as proud to have sat down for your morning devotion or evening workout? It's there. In the heart of us all, a battle of pride wages and if we're not careful, it can leak out and destroy those we say we care about.

Have you ever been asked this question: Who, in all of history, would you want to meet and what would you ask them? I'm currently reading *The Dinner List* by Rebecca Serle. The main character's roommate once asked her to write a list of five people, dead or alive, she'd invite to a dinner party. Years of experience, loss and love later, she happens upon her birthday dinner with all of those individuals waiting for her. It's wild and thoughtful and I couldn't help wonder who my five would be. I probably gave this idea and embarrassing amount of my time, but I know for sure that one would be Paul. Is it so lame or obvious that I'd choose a Biblical person? A close second to him is Justin Bieber but for a hundred different reasons. Regardless, he's in my top five.

Originally named Saul of Tarsus, Paul first makes his appearance in the New Testament book of Acts, where we discover traits of the early church. He was a dictating Roman Citizen who I would classify today as a terrorist. He ravaged through cities, binding and killing men and women who proclaimed a faith in Jesus. When he and two others were in pursuit of greater persecution in Damascus, a town north of Israel towards Lebanon,

Scripture tells us he was blinded by a bright light that spoke, *Why are you persecuting me?* We learn that it is God who greets him and blinds him, but the thing is, we're almost convinced that Saul, because of his choices, doesn't know God. But in that moment, we see that in fact, he calls him *Lord* (Acts 9:5). God instructs him from there, to continue to Damascus, assuring a safe place to rest. Likewise, he calls to a man, Ananais, and tells him to look for Saul and bring him in. Imagine, for a moment, the reputation preceding Saul when he arrives in Damascus. How many times did he sit through agonizing conversations with people, assuring them of who he was now, the choices he was making differently, and his regret over leading others to their punishment or death? How many times would villagers flee from his presence out of fear of what they had heard he'd done before? Others fearing their own reputation by associating themselves with him.

    We often look at the twelve disciples that are known for being with Jesus during his ministry before and just after his death and resurrection. What an honor. They witnessed miracles on the ocean, while they sat to eat, and while they walked between towns. They heard Jesus and saw Him and knew Him by name. And then there's Peter, who isn't on my top five list but is worth the mention. A disciple who denies Jesus over and over and over again, you have my attention. What is more, before Jesus even calls Peter as a disciple He knew that Peter would eventually deny Him. The account of Peter's denial is in all four of the gospels, Matthew, Mark, Luke and John. The first four books of the New Testament share about the wonders of Jesus, but also the widely known truth in all of humanity- choice.

    Back to Saul, whose name was changed to Paul during his ministry, who in his thirty something years of teaching the power and hope of Jesus, is attributed to writing thirteen books in the New Testament, all of which speak to the church, to persecution, and to the power of the resurrection that he knows quite well. We learn that Paul's knowledge of God grew from an impersonal belief, to a multi-generational, international impact for Christ. His ministry started from the ragged destruction of a broken soul- his broken soul.

My question to Paul would be this, *How long did it take you to forgive yourself, and accept God's forgiveness?* Ok, I cheated. It's a two-for.

I can't put that baby back in my womb but I can hope that through my story and vulnerability God will do great things. Shoot, He's already doing great things. The fact that you're reading this is proof of that. He restores us. Shards of glass become a masterpiece. Broken stories become a book of healing. And through it all, our Maker is seen. Our Crafter is appreciated. It's not that I didn't know Christ. I did. I still do. I have all along. But what I did not fully understand was the depravity of my own sin that separated me from God. I didn't know how truly desperate I was to be found in my Savior until I was succumb by the greatness of my need for Him.

CHAPTER NINE: THE FLESH OF MERCY

Fear can convince us to do just about anything. Ask any journalist, politician or mother whose kid has a food allergy. Some precious friends of ours have two squeezable nugget boys. The older son has severe, multiple food allergies, requiring epipens, strict intake regiments, and many, many visits out of town for specialists. This mama friend and I have sat in her home, in mine, along the shore of a lake, and continuously she walks me through what their restrictions are, what mild to severe symptoms look like, and how it has fully infiltrated their home and their lives. When their second son was born last summer, the pediatrician gave them a food introduction schedule that began around four months. After introducing the first few food groups, results were clear. The narrative looked different and there were no symptoms indicating allergens. For the first time in years, these cherished friends took breaths of freedom, but it didn't last long.

Last month, her husband was downtown for work and she was home alone with their boys. She had just put them down for afternoon naps and within minutes, the baby became violently ill, losing color and consciousness too quickly. She was tirelessly on the phone between 911 and her husband who was rushing home from his real estate office. She attempted two epipens, but neither one gave him more than a few crying seconds. It wasn't working. Without hesitation or shoes, she bolted out of their home, down the cement steps, clutching their limp baby into her chest. She ran to the neighbors who she knew were first responders. In a robe, worn like a cape of bravery, in fear of losing their child, she fought with everything she had.

Through the evening, she'd send messages and photo updates from the Emergency Room. She fought with nurses to see her preferred physician. She fought for the tests she knew he'd need. She fought for the attention to their son. She prayed and called our community to prayer. Their son was discharged the next day and has made a merciful recovery. I'm not saying that when you fight with all you've got, you'll get the outcome you so desperately desire. But I am saying that fear induces action we never thought we were capable of.

    Remember the college counselor I told you about? The one who encouraged the path of healing from my childhood? Understand the gravity of that relationship. God gave her our names and she took us in. She never withheld perspective, challenge or patience, regardless of how many times us girls would hesitate to let her in. In my last year of college, her son passed away from an inoperable brain tumor. The symptoms came on quickly and it was awful to witness the decline of life. I so badly wanted to give her the perfect words and balanced emotions, to be there with her through it all. But the association to that kind of grief was unbearable and uncomfortable, and slowly I made it about myself. I'd justify my lack of response with excuses. She had other friends and family support and certainly didn't need my presence in her living room. I didn't know how to be present without being consumed by emotion, and for some reason, that seemed negative to me. The idea of valuing and loving someone so much, seeing them in their pain and stepping in with them, was foreign, so I opted out. Pulling back and sending text messages instead of standing at her door or crying in ache with her.

When I saw my positive pee stick, it affirmed the fears I had rooted into my belief system. The fear that again I was finding myself in the middle of a mess I didn't know how to get out of. I wasn't married or engaged. I wasn't even dating the guy anymore. I didn't have my own home or a full-time job with any type of benefits. There was nothing secure about my lifestyle other than my love for Nordstrom Rack. I just graduated from college and barely felt like an adult. I couldn't be a mom. And this baby wouldn't have a dad. The level of conclusions I came to because of fear and isolation led to the greatest decision I'd forever regret. And I didn't need a group of people preaching politics or conservative persecution at me for something I already knew I wished I hadn't done.

After the abortion, I sank to the lowest of lows. The greatest depth and darkness that covers the bottom of sea. There I laid. I stopped responding to messages and phone calls. No motivation to continue on for a Masters degree. My stomach was empty without the ache for food. Nothing could fill it. The grief and ache were unbearable. But who could I tell who would just listen? Did I even want to tell someone? How would I start that conversation? How could I admit my floundering to anyone and hope for respite? But when it all broke open and I had no other choice but to address the truth in front of me, one friend sat there, giving me the space I craved and feared. She listened to as many of the details I was willing to share. She listened to me apologize for lying to her. She let me cry the ugly tears, even the embarrassingly snotty ones. She didn't have perfectly sorted through words to respond. She didn't offer me her emotions. It felt unbalanced and uncomfortable. But what mattered more than feeling uncomfortable, was knowing she was there. When she took the time to sit and listen, offering solace, she spoke more than any word ever could have. Believe me, it wasn't easy on her end. She had been lied to and deceived. Her association to my mess was nothing to boast about. But she was there.

After what seemed like a billion minutes on the fringe of wondering what Eric would choose, he invited me into his home and washed my feet. I was sure it would be a deal breaker from the get-go, which was why I gave him the same lie of having had a miscarriage. That was enough for him to take in when we first started dating, so imagine if you will having to recalculate facts and terms and emotions with the truth. Nothing about his choice to trust me and my character was easy for him but somewhere in those moments, clutching to the surety of Jesus, he forgave me for lying and later that year we were married. Not out of pity. Not out of obligation. Not to be a hero. But because of love. His presence and forgiveness spoke mercy to my soul. And the gift of grace was for us both.

    The week after my friend's baby was in the hospital, she was slow to respond to messages. She didn't answer her phone calls. The spiral of grief had set in, and I knew this introversion. The pressure we put on ourselves to be fine. The emotional catapult into solitude. The rejection of others and their offerings. So when Eric came home from teaching one night, I grabbed a bottle of wine, a bag of chocolate, bubbly water, and met her at her door. It was well past bedtime but I knew she'd be up. We were unhinged-both in our pajamas, not a shred of makeup or cute hair. *I can't look at that fireplace without seeing my lifeless boy.* There was trauma. Grief. A mother's heartache, still spiraling. And she didn't need my words, although we talked and cried and I listened until the wee morning hours. There was nothing perfectly poised about it, but from what I know, from where I've been and from what I've learned, there is holiness in presence. The late Dutch writer and theologian, Henri Nouwen said this:

The friend who can be silent with us in a moment of despair or confusion, who can stay with us in an hour of grief and bereavement, who can tolerate not knowing … not healing, not curing … that is a friend who cares.

Sitting with someone in their mess, in their grief, when we allow presence, trusted presence, truth and love and mercy, the destructive influence of Satan is powerless. Love is the gift that draws others out of isolation.

Abortion is so, incredibly isolating. As is parenting with food allergies. And mothering in general. Sitting in grief. Standing in success. Isolation hits regardless of social economy, status, gender, race or sin.

I think about Jesus at the Well in the New Testament book of John. In chapter 4, we're given a picture of Jesus, tired from His trek to Galilee. He and His disciples stopped to rest in Samaria. His disciples went in to town for food while Jesus sat by the well. We're told there's a Samaritan woman there and Jesus, being a Jew, asked her for a drink. Shocked that Jesus would even talk to her because of her social status, she responds this way, *How is it that you, a Jew, ask for a drink from me?* They go back and forth about the analogy of living water, and what God provides as a gift for her. Knowing already who she is because Jesus is the King of Sovereignty, He asked her to call for her husband. She responds that she does not have one and Jesus replies:

You are right in saying, 'I have no husband'; for you have had five husbands, and the one you now have is not your husband. What you have said is true.

The woman knows this is a prophet and that He is the chosen Messiah. What's more, when she shares with others in her town about Jesus and how He knew her, others came to believe.

Jesus didn't show up with a crew of mighty horsemen and fancy suede shoes. He wasn't the picture of a hero, if that's what your picture of a hero is. An Elvis and William Wallace blend who was also capable of ninja skills. He was exhausted when he sat by the well. He could have gone into town with the disciples for food, I'm sure that man was hungry. But He saw her and He knew her, and He knew that she needed His presence. I like to think they went there just for her- that even on their way, He knew exactly what and where they were going and it wasn't a detour, but a destination. I like to think that because God knows all, He also knew that one day I'd read that text and it would level me out.

I feared what others would think of me. I feared their words, their judgements and their stares. I feared my reputation and my future. I feared being the outcast. Then I grieved a life. And I grieved a death. I grieved until my soul could ache no more. And then a friend sat with me. And she listened. And she threw off the worry of association and comfort. She knew I needed to know that I was deeply loved still. And she loved me in the best way she knew how. And then Eric washed my feet and began giving me space to rebuild. I can only hope that God uses me to build others in those moments when they need kindness the most. That kind of mercy is God in the flesh and it casts out isolation and fear.

CHAPTER TEN: GUTS AND GRIT OF PTSD

Before going to publish, I wrestled and rolled through this chapter more than any other. Well, the About the Author part turned me upside down. Somehow I can write a whole book about my story but get twisted and caught in the one paragraph summary about what else I want you to know about me. What is necessary?

This chapter though, came a close second but for different reasons. My parents own a non-profit organization in the South Bay Area, utilizing equine therapy for children and adults with special needs. In the last few years, this organization has expanded to a partnership with the V.A. Weekly, my folks host a group of veterans. Some ride. Others walk the horses. Some muck stalls. Some come out to observe. A few of the men are homeless. Many of the women have abusive stories of their own. All of them associate with trauma.

I've been up to my gut, nervous to use these letters and the term, but I can't fully tell my story without it. So here it is, or here they are. PTSD. If you're unaware of what that stands for, it's Post-Traumatic Stress Disorder. Growing up in a wide-cast Air Force family, witnessing the veteran program within my folks' non-profit, and sitting with friends who have lost a loved one from modern warfare, my association to this term has settled there, with war and military veterans. The witnessing of traumatic mass shootings in our country would also fall under this category, but not me. Not someone who was a young target of molestation. Not someone who voluntarily terminated their pregnancy.

When a counselor we've been seeing on and off for five or so years, recommended trauma therapy, I had not considered anything in my life qualifying as PTSD and felt completely unsettled that he would suggest this. Weekly, for months, this counselor encouraged and offered multiple mental exercises to unravel the unseen components of my story- the years of nightmares and sweat-ridden pillow cases, the self-sabotaging behavior in my relationships and the stiffness that would come with specific sounds. News to me, but all of those align with stress due to trauma.

Once I allowed myself to see it all for what it was, healing felt closer than it ever had before. Prior to trauma counseling, I'd cast it off as an emotional narrative, continuing to bury myself under the graves of isolation. But I believe God used that counselor to help me understand the greater *why*. *My greater why*. It didn't matter how confident I was in my faith despite abortion if I wasn't addressing the punishment I put myself through because of trauma. It didn't matter how often I'd be open to sharing my story if I still lived in the timid shame of a ten year old.

If I really desired God to restore me, and I did, then I'd have to let Him expose me, all of me. The ugliest parts. The hidden parts. The greatest parts of who I was. I'd have to see it all too, and to do that, I'd have to be willing to get ahold of my *crazy, ruined self*. Thanks Anne.

One of our go-to marital arguments is because someone apologized for something they aren't actually owning. How can you really be sorry for something you don't acknowledge having done? Sure, you can apologize for unknowingly offending me, but if there is no corroboration over the actual action and a point of resolve, why apologize?

Similarly, how can you be healed from something that you aren't aware needs mending? I knew my faith was strong and I could address the facts- I was abused and I had an abortion, but the internal symptoms of hesitation, restraint, a lack of trust, were all stems of trauma. As long as that went unacknowledged, the symptoms populated.

Trauma has a name but it doesn't have to have victory over your life. If you, or someone you love, is struggling with PTSD, please get help. You're worth it. Your story isn't over.

CHAPTER ELEVEN: A BIT FAMILIAR

Fertility, man. It is a thing. We have countless friends who have struggled and some who are still steadying the course of conception in hopes of having just one biological baby. I've been on the other end of a phone call, hearing heart ache as another friend says, *I started my period. We'll see again next month.* They've been in and out of doctor's offices, counseling sessions, chiropractic visits, acupuncture and acupressure appointments. They've undergone surgeries and an annoying amount of advice. They've prayed hard and angrily. They've watched friends and sisters and neighbors announce a new or another pregnancy. They've joined in the celebration, welcoming new life with the utmost of humility. And from where I stand, they deserve a family- a whole fleet of squishy babies.

Before Abby was born, I was working full time in the prevention field. Our primary aim was education, and with that, comes ... you guessed it, conferences! Always conferences. We held and attended conferences, both local and state-wide, some by phone, some within the school systems, all with the aim of strategizing drug, alcohol and suicide prevention among teenagers. With the participation in hundreds of student's lives, also came child protective services calls and visits, chauffeuring students to and from school, dances and probation meetings. I'd watch these students suffer from disengagement, disenfranchisement and feeling incomplete and unlovable. Jointly I'd hear friends in their struggle for fertility and think, *God, how does this make sense that some of these parents don't care for their kids, while others go to the extreme lengths just for the opportunity to be a parent?*

During our first year of marriage, Eric and I were driving to the Bay Area for a friend's wedding and I just couldn't seem to keep my eyes open. I laid my whole body back in our white Subaru's passenger seat. I was equal parts hungry and nauseous and it felt just a bit familiar. By the time we arrived, I had considered it. After I threw up for the second time in the reception bathroom, I knew. Eric was equally elated and terrified. It wasn't planned and felt too soon. We weren't even married a full year, and at that point, it had only been two years since the abortion and though this narrative was different, I was afraid.

I was afraid to claim it. Not the baby- I knew it was mine. But to claim a gift that I didn't feel like I deserved when so many others were trying so desperately. It all felt embarrassing and I didn't know how to be joyful.

On our way home we stopped at Urban Outfitters, because isn't that the first place you think of for baby items? Eric found a small white bunny-like stuffed animal with short stumpy legs that almost resembled a pig. Eric, to this day, tells me it was a bunny. I say pig.

Marriage is fun. It was the exact thing you'd expect to find at Urban Outfitters and oddly cute enough to name it *baby's first toy*. For the days that followed, I battled hard against the pretense that I didn't deserve this baby. I had told myself that because I forfeited my chance at motherhood on that day in June, I didn't deserve another. Within the week I started bleeding and at our doctor's appointment a few days later, it was made clear that I was no longer pregnant. *See this, this is what I deserve.* I wanted to be sad and I was sad, but expressing my sorrow felt shameful. After all, I didn't deserve this baby anyway, right? I didn't deserve the gift of motherhood or a chance for redemption. Isn't that what we hear and settle into, that God's wrath punishes sinners?

    A few weeks ago, my almost seven year old punched her sister in the face and then lied to me when I asked her for the truth. I was folding laundry in my bedroom, just across the hallway from their shared room. I heard it- the sound of a clenched fist to a nose. Abby met me in the hallway, holding her face while she compiled herself enough between sobs to explain what happened. Immediately Izzy rushed out and without question said, *I didn't do anything. She walked into my fist.* As thought the lie would hold up with the bucket of evidence. Lord have mercy on mothers everywhere.

Consoling Abby for those next few minutes, my anger was fuming. As I hugged her I also strategized Izzy's discipline.

> *Would I take away friend time? TV shows? Dessert for that whole week?*
>
> *Was I going to collect all of her toys and donate them to a local charity?*
>
> *Or better yet, have her collect them all and walk them in, stating the reason for such punishment?*
>
> *Would a spanking do anything for her since she's almost my height and it takes*

every inch of woman-power in me to hold her down.

Oh I was mad. I sent Abby down the hall with Finley, our youngest, to be entertained by Octonauts while I closed the bedroom door, locking us in. Three hundred thoughts rushed passed me. Long pause. When I opened my eyes, I breathed in, said a quiet plea of desperation and leaned in close so she knew just how serious I was. We talked about lying and hitting and how none of that is acceptable behavior. There's a say in our house, *Mom can handle the truth*. I repeated that to her when she tried to lie to me again. She was disciplined and hated it, and probably hated me in those moments of pain. She screamed at me and as much as I wanted to run out of the house, tapping out to Eric, I sat there. She wiggled around like a snake in a wading pool, but I held her and whispered, *I love you*.

Discipline could have looked one hundred and sixty percent different that day had it been extended with the intent of harm. My intention was not wrath, but instruction. To teach her boundaries and to help her understand how our actions affect others. My job as her parent is not only to lay the groundwork of obedience but also to advocate for grace.

Do things happen in our world and in our lives as consequences of our sin? Certainly. But does God intend harm when He's teaching us His grace? God didn't force my miscarriage as His wrath against me because of my sin, or at least I don't believe that. The miscarriage, I believe, was a natural consequence because sin entered our world long ago. The God I believe in says, *You are forgiven because you have asked for forgiveness.* The God who rolled back the stone and proved Himself as King and Conquerer three days after His death on the cross, who is able to resurrect us into holiness with Him, is also the one who David, a man after God's own heart, declared redeems us from the pit.

The Lord is merciful and gracious, slow to anger and abounding in steadfast love ... He does not deal with us according to our sins, nor repay us according to our iniquities ... as far as the east is from the west, so far does he remove our transgressions from us ... as a father shows compassion to his children, so the Lord shows compassion to those who fear him.
   Psalm 4:8-13

A good friend of mine is an 8 on the Enneagram. If you know this, you know her tendencies well. Strong and stubborn, self-confident and decisive. Without hesitation, when someone comments, *I deserved this*, or *I didn't deserve that*, she replies, *No, you deserve death*. We all laugh every time, partly because empathy is not her natural gift but also because it's true. Our sin, our words and actions that separate us from God deserves death, but because of the grave, because of what Jesus did, by taking our sins to the cross with Him on the hill of Calvary, the hill He created, the final eternal payment for us, He resurrected each and every one of us from the dead with power and mercy in his hands. His life for ours. His pain for our redemption.

When insecurity in my faith told me that I didn't deserve that baby anyway, a redemptive God says otherwise.

CHAPTER TWELVE: MY ARK

I used to read the story of Noah and the Ark, and from hearing it all those years as a kid in Sunday School, it became a fable. A fairy tale with a glorified ending. An idyllic story with animated giraffes and zebras, sailing the seven seas in search of an olive branch. Somewhere between six year old me and thirty year old me, details became muffled and muted, but every time God says, *Share your story*, I think of Noah.

When God told Noah to build the ark and gather animals, what was he responsible for? Building the ark and gathering animals. People mocked him and disbelieved that God was instructing him. There was a severe drought in the land and surely no rain would come. About four years into our married life here in Sonora, the rain and snow dried up and there was a drought. The grey winter skies looked promising, even the trickles of precipitation. But no rain. No snow. For consecutive years, the local water companies limited basic usage and set outrageous overage fees. The ground and air and my skin demanded moisture.

God didn't instruct Noah to convince his community that rain was coming. God didn't expect Noah to cause the rain, stop the rain, or even provide dry land. I don't even think Noah was told to get a contractor's license or the permits to build such a large wooden structure. But I do believe that somewhere in the heart of Noah, he heard God and believed Him.

That afternoon in San Diego, when this friend of a friend learned she was pregnant, God said, *Share your story*. He didn't say, *Build her a crib* or *Convince her this way or that*. He didn't tell me to protest or create legislation. He didn't even give me hope for an outcome. He didn't promise me ease. He invited me into obedience and out from hiding. The outcome was less than desirable for the months that followed. I felt forsaken, alone and angry. Betrayed, even. But hope has sprung as I have seen God's design in the greater rooting of my faith.

    During the parent orientation before Izzy started Kindergarten, we gathered in the school's multi-purpose room. Some people can saunter in all FBI and Secret Service like, scanning the room with slyness. I've never had that stealth. You will know when I'm looking. I can't balance the duration of my stares. My apologies. I sat at a long, rectangular table along the right side of the room with a few friends who were also new to this school. As I looked to my left, there was a blonde, similar in height and stature to me but with way cuter clothes, standing next to what I presumed was her husband, tall and an obvious cowboy. I had no idea who their kid was or what grade they were there for. I didn't know if they grew up here or were transplants, like myself, to this small town, but I hoped that we'd be friends. Do you ever see someone and just want to know them? Or at least hope they don't dislike you? Shortly after the school administration and teacher's introductions, the Principal gave a brief informative speech and sent us out to visit our children's classrooms. As I walked across the basketball courts, towards the Kinder yard, there they were, the Blonde and the Cowboy, heading straight for where I was headed.

    For those next few weeks, we'd smile at each other during school drop off. Younger siblings trailed along with us and at pick-up, as they played tag, it seemed natural but mostly necessary to introduce ourselves. I learned that her name was Claire. Not really, but for the book she is Claire. Day by day our conversations grew from short to remembered, nap time advice to friendship. At one point she learned that I blog and asked what I write about. I was still trying to figure that out myself. I had started a new blog, mainly motherhood related, so I gave her a handful of topics from that. Maybe it was the next day or week, but during pick-up, as we stood between boulders and oak trees, watching our younger kids run in leaves, she asked if she could share one of my posts with her friend.

Claire didn't share any of the *why* details with me, and I didn't ask, but I was glad nonetheless and felt encouraged she even read through my stories of mishaps and advice. I didn't hesitate the *yes* and then the big kids came out, we went home and somehow months flew by like only time does, and we found ourselves at her son's birthday party. We sat in our REI lawn chairs, watching as the hoard of kids ran zigzags between a super hero themed bounce house, the swing set and the horses that her son calls his.

About an hour later, as Eric was loading our chairs and the kid's sweatshirts into the Sienna, I stood back with another mom anticipating the hilariousness of what was to come. Claire's Cowboy lined the kids up youngest to oldest, with Finley (our baby child) near the front of the crew. Have you ever watched a new-to-two year old try to hold a metal bat, let alone accurately swing it at a moving target? Thank you Jesus for the humor in parenting. I couldn't contain myself or the chuckles out of my mouth, and caught the eye of this soon-to-be mom friend rocking next to me with her Ergo infant. I rarely make the first move and introduce myself out of nowhere, not because I don't care to, but because I will mess up my words and the introvert will slowly die inside of my soul. Happens every time. But because of our eye lock, it would have been more odd to then, un-acknowledge her. So there I was, shaking hands and petting her baby like the best politician, and as I said my name, she stopped me with this, *So I know who you are*. I didn't know whether to thank her or apologize, coward down and run, or smile. So my eyes just got big and my grin got bigger and my teeth started to sputter. I'm convinced that's the only moment in my life where time literally stood still and I stared, zombie like at her for what seemed like eleven minutes. It's very likely she noticed my glazed over, panicked face and continued, *Claire told me to read your blog. I'm Lou.* Dots connected. So this was the friend.

Me: *Oh, ok! It's so great to meet you. How old is your baby?*

Lou: *She's six months. So a couple of months ago I called Claire in a panic. We already have three kids and this one is still a baby. We didn't want more, so when we found out I was pregnant again, we didn't know what to do.*

Me: *Ok.*

Lou: *After a couple of days, my husband and I decided to abort the baby. We just couldn't financially and mentally handle one more kid. I made my appointment but still felt unsettled about it. Claire encouraged me to read your blog post, the one about your abortion story. I didn't want to. I didn't want a political or religious sway.*

But my husband and I got into a fight one night and I couldn't sleep, so I read it.

Me: *Oh, thank you.*

Lou: *You didn't tell me not to make this choice. You didn't tell me to be a Christian or a Conservative. You told your story. The next morning I called and cancelled the appointment. I just don't think I could have lived with the guilt of it all.*

Me: *(sobbing into my shoulder while the kids still bash said piñata) Wow. I don't know what to say.*

Lou: *Thank you for telling your story.*

Me: *(still silently wiping tear streams off my cheeks) Thank you.*

It took me months to write the blog post she read. For the first time I had told my story in a very public and social arena. What if someone read it and blasted me because I wasn't taking a firm political stance? What if, once again, my character is called to question and I'm found struggling to prove something? I hesitated over and over again. I found every possible distraction and dish to clean before I'd sit to write. I'd write and write and then delete it all. I started a seventy times, each time fighting against fear and doubt and isolation. God still asked me to share it. He didn't back down even when I did. Then I wrote and wrote and didn't delete. Friends who knew I was writing it, checked in to make sure I didn't give up. I edited and revised and published. God didn't promise me a certain outcome. He didn't promise that I wouldn't doubt. He didn't make promises on proving my character. Sometimes He calls us into obedience for the sole purpose of surrender.

    This story is my story and it's been given by Him. It's a story of love and He asked me to share it. Sharing my story led to weekly posts from others willing to share theirs in order to connect with others who needed to come out of the dark places. From losing a child to finances and parenting endeavors, we had the gamut. I had hoped it would at least last one month, posting weekly. It took us through Easter. For four months, every week, women braved vulnerability and gave thousands of readers the hope of release. I had no idea that the blogging platform would be used for that. I had no idea who would rally and champion these stories. I had no idea He was carving a life to be lived, to be saved, and I got to be a part of it. I had no idea that He was calling people out from their financial stress because one friend offered her story of struggle and success.

Noah built that gigantic cypress ark and filled it to its breaching brim with livestock, mammals, birds and bunnies. Every animal, clean and unclean, males and females. Just as he was asked. The rain didn't come immediately but when it did, it covered the earth. God did just as He said He would.

The promise is and has always been in Him alone. That winter, when I finally shared my story, it rained. It actually rained so hard here, for so long, that it flooded streets and front yards and creek beds. What a promise of hope!

CHAPTER THIRTEEN: BEYOND THE 'A' WORDS

I recently had a friend ask me how I forgave the person who molested me. She and her daughter were over for a lunch playdate and as the girls played in the backyard, we were inside making sandwiches and cutting watermelon. I had been recounting a recent story to her of being in the same room with that person and about ten other people. I said it casually and brushed passed it, trying not to give details as to who that person was. A few minutes later, the kids rushed in to eat and about eleven minutes later, had plowed through the food and were begging to get back outside to their spy game. My mind had already shifted to clean up mode, clearing the plastic plates and putting the ranch dressing bottle away in the fridge, but my friend jumped us back to that comment. I also realize that you're probably wondering why we had the ranch dressing out for sandwiches and watermelon and it's because my youngest will put that tasty trash on just about anything. Back to the story …

Wait. So you were just there with him?
Do you see him a lot?
How do you even stand to be there?

Please let it be known that abuse is never okay. It will never be okay. Not in any environment or circumstance, anywhere, ever. I stand firm on that. Being one who was abused, however, I have a choice. For years and years it dictated my breathing, my emotions and my story. It affected every relationship I had because it disqualified my purity and my voice as the other half. There was baggage. Heavy baggage. I brashly judged myself and others, drawing and assuming conclusions and outcomes. Every bad decision and correct assumption was blamed on him or me and those experiences I wish I never had. The law I created of victimization built a case against God and every time I'd feel the slightest insecurity, it was one more notch in my strong belt as to why God didn't protect me and didn't, in fact, care for me.

Until I made a choice that turned me inside out. Remember the chapter on The Shack? Well, when I finally read it I was hunched at the feet of God, weeping on the bathroom floor. My family called it the airplane bathroom because it was that small- tucked away in the laundry room. My whole body barely fit on the ground between the toilet and sink, but there I was, head over feet as I wept. Loud and unhinged with The Shack in my hands. It was after the abortion when I was still in the lie but I thought back to the drive downtown after meeting Bob. I thought about what God had asked of me. I thought about the questions my dad asked me after I exposed the truth to he and my mom.

How much longer, Em?
How much longer will you run from me?

How much longer will you refuse ownership over your life and over your story?
I have more for you.
Don't you trust me?
I didn't want this for you either, but we all have a choice and that was his.
You have made choices too and want to be forgiven.
I have made promises for you and you can trust me.

I didn't want my story and I fought hand and fist at God over it. Like I said earlier, I didn't want to be the girl abused. I didn't want to be the girl who couldn't trust others. I didn't want to be the person others couldn't trust. I didn't want to be the girl who hid behind the smile and the lies. And I didn't want to be the girl who got pregnant and had an abortion. I didn't want her story. But I'm guessing Paul didn't want his story either. Or Peter. Or the woman at the well. I'm guessing there are parts of your story you don't want to claim. I'm guessing Jesus didn't really want to have to die that way- gruesome and bloody on the cross. How much easier for Him would it have been to die in His sleep? To not feel anything and wake up in the clouds. Just to have God take Him away into the Heavenly spaces where He existed before. I was so focused on my past that it became a leech, sucking up my whole story. I thought it was the end of my story and I never considered what could be possible beyond the brokenness. When I started being honest and open to sharing my whole story, whether finally in counseling, in my marriage, with young groups of middle school or high school students, or with people I didn't know, God reminded me that my story didn't end in shame. It didn't end in fear. It didn't even end with exposure to the light. It was my fears that were broken and faulty, not me.

You see, I was focused on the whole narrative of brokenness that I didn't fully understand that there was wholeness waiting. That in fact, my whole story is the greatest love story every told. It's your story too. It's the story of a perfect and kind, loving and forgiving Savior stepping into every mess we'd ever make, before we took our first breath, being with us as we learn and grow, and rescuing us into the perfectly present peace that only comes through Him. It doesn't come easily though. It comes with knowing that we will screw it up. It's what we do best. But it also comes with His sacrifice to love us despite just how screwy we are.

    I recently finished reading my first Jodi Picoult book, *A Spark of Light*. We were flying to Washington for a cousin's wedding and the day before we left, I took the kids to one of our smaller public libraries just up the highway to return their summer reading books. We hadn't planned on checking out new books until we returned the following week, but there was a display of adult fiction books and I am one hundred percent the person who judges a book by its cover. The vibrancy and stark white font captured me. I had never read any of her books and you guys, I didn't even read the back cover or inlay to see what it was about. But it came home with me and joined us on the flight and in my hotel room. I couldn't put it down. She crafts the story of an extreme anti-abortionist taking a clinic hostage. The pages unravel the lives and back-stories of those engaged in this hostile situation. It is ruthless at times, eery and too familiar with some of the details. Details I had long forgotten, or at least tried to forget. But she says this and it stuck with me,

> *The most ardent antis didn't realize how many women they knew who's had an abortion. Wipe away the stigma and all you were left with was your neighbor, your teacher, your grocery clerk, your landlady.*

A few years ago I shared my story with a group of middle school girls per the request of a friend who knew my life. That night, Eric and I were watching some Food Network show, probably Master Chef because we are here for the crazy that comes with British chef

Gordon Ramsay. My phone buzzed and it was the mom of one of the girls in that earlier evening group. She wanted to set up a time to meet and I threw my head back with nerves that I'd, for sure, be yelled at. The parents probably didn't know that their daughters would be hearing about an abortion. Maybe they just expected a G rated sex-like story, if there is one, and this would be the first of many phone calls I was sure to get, offering shock and despise.

Two days later, I drove like a sloth through town, kids in tow, to their home. I thought that if our conversation became too heated, impending nap time would be the perfect get-out-of-there charm. I readied myself the best I could with Bieber tunes and deep breaths. I had heard it all, even on my wedding day, so bring it on. As our kids played between the staircase (because what else do toddlers gravitate towards if not danger), she offered me tea and we sat at their Pottery Barn farmhouse kitchen table. It took no more than two minutes for her to dive in and I was five thousand percent shocked when she apologized to having heard my story from their daughter. She continued that her daughter was especially impacted by my honesty and in turn, she shared her own story of having had an abortion. This mom unfolded years of being alone and feeling isolated in her shame. Her story was over ten years ago, yet the number of people she had let in up to that point could be counted on one hand.

Within the first year of openly sharing my full story, three friends of mine also shared with me that they had abortions. I never would have placed them in a line up. These are all well-loving mothers and wives, stand-out participants in our communities. Remove the stereotype and the stigma and what you have are your friends. Tried and true and full of honor. Equipped with grace and mercy and humility. We are in your churches, trusted to teach your children in schools. We attend MOPS and are directors of programming. Camp counselors. On supervising boards, school boards, church staff. We are moms and sisters, daughters and friends.

Aphesis- we are released. I knew this word would come up again and I'm glad it did. It so perfectly pulls together the fullness of freedom. We have been offered the abundant gift of this freedom- this unwavering love. Beyond the abuse and abortion, I live. And so do you. Beyond whatever story in your life holds you back, you are released. May you, this day, live in the light of being free.

SECTION THREE: LETTERS OF **A**BSOLUTION

CHAPTER FOURTEEN: TO THE VICTORS

I want to cue Panic at the Disco's *Victorious* song here as you read this letter. It is with the greatest hope that I'm not the first one encouraging you to live out your whole story. I hope for your hope. I hope for your recovery. I hope for your healing and your solace as you are found in the wholeness of who God made you to be. And no one (NO ONE) can take that away from you.

Recently I attended an annual fundraising event for my folks' non-profit. This specific event is dedicated to the veterans assistance program and year after year, this fundraiser sells out, expanding to larger facilities. And it's no wonder. The speakers are those in the program who wish to tell their story and the affects of healing from the equine program. You'd think the greatest expense would be tissues because there is not one tearless person sitting at those farm tables. This year, as a retired Army veteran shared her story of being molested on base, she paused and invited those who've been the target of trauma to stand with her. It was the single most powerful moment of the whole evening. There, in an open-space ranch setting, she used the pain of her story to rescue others out of their damning and condemning darkness.

You are in her story. A part of it anyway, witnessing and remembering and daring to change the coordinates of how you treat others, raise others and see others. You have the grit of empathy and the concern of love.

This book wouldn't be complete without that part of the story. I hesitated writing it for fear I'd give a tell to who it was- again, protecting that person and hiding in a different part of the story. Thankfully, a dear friend encouraged me to steady the course. She reminded me of all the people who needed to finally live acquitted in their own skin, in their own stories. Though filled with trauma, we are found in freedom.

This is for you. These words. The healing. The forgiving. The trust that God has a perfect purpose in all of it and that you and I get to be a part of whatever that is. This is just the beginning, my friends. May we run today as victors, not victims.

CHAPTER FIFTEEN: TO THOSE WITH THE "A" IN THEIR STORY

Some of you, I've had the privilege of meeting. We've shared tea in my living room. We've sat at your kitchen table while the kids jumped around like baboons. You've cried alone for many, many years. You've wondered what your child would be like, what you would have been like as a mom then. We've shared our fears and regrets and the sorrow in it all.

Others of you, I have not yet met but I see you. I know you're there, on the other side of these pages. Maybe everyone knows your story too. There's a chance some of you are still living isolated with your experience because you fear that no one would understand. You fear failure and confrontation.

No one tells you how to process it and unfortunately, there's a stigma anyways that pushes comfort away. Maybe some of you were even told to just move on, as though it was nothing. Not a life and loss to grieve. Maybe you feel guilty, like I did, to mourn and stake claim of your emotions.

I remember being in our first year of marriage and I'd startle myself awake from the nightmares of that room. I'd flinch at the closing of a metal garbage can lid that took me right back to laying partially coherent as my baby died. The repercussions of that trauma were undeniable.

Sometimes I think the baby was a boy. There's nothing of proof for that belief, but I just think it was. For the longest time, I was embarrassed to admit that. It felt like because I forfeited that chance of mothering, I couldn't claim the child. I couldn't feel everything I was feeling. But friends, I do, I think that baby would have been a boy and every December, I think of what would have been a birthday celebration.

You have permission to mourn, do you know that? You have permission to tell someone and not live in isolation. You have permission to miss that baby and claim it.

Hear it now. Today, you are meant to live in freedom because that's what our King has done for you when He came to life out of the tomb. Claim the freedom today, friends and release yourself into the favor of Goodness.

CHAPTER SIXTEEN: TO MY DAUGHTERS

This was never the story I wanted to tell you but it is my story. What's more, it's the story of how God brought me to my knees in reverence to His mercy. But just because this is how He got my attention, doesn't mean it's how He needs to get yours. Your story, regardless of what you choose, starts and ends with Him. When you were just a thought, just a hope in my heart of hearts, He knew you and crafted you and called you by name. Daughter of the King. It's the best kind of name. It roots you in the eternal Father, considers you heiresses in His kingdom, and grants you access to your Maker. It's far better than the name your dad and I chose for you, though we picked some good ones!

Sisters. I love you all more and more than you know. This book was written with you in mind. It's for you today, as mere toddlers and elementary school kids figuring out the ways of friendship and trust and your own conscience. As you play *Marco-Pillow* in Grandma and Papa's pool, embracing all that is pure in your little lives. It's here for you in your teenage years when you press and bud and revolt against boundaries of identity and love and grace. It's for when you fly away from our nest and pursue who you are- your gifts, your talents and passions, your relationships outside of the safety net of supervision. I hope and pray for your confidence to be established in He who knows and carries you. In who designed you and delights in your every breath. I hope that you know you always have a room, a cup of tea, and a warm hug waiting. My grace and love go with you wherever you are.

You are never without a place in this world. May His light guide you every step of the way.

xo

Mom

AN **A**FTERWARD OF THOUGHTS

While writing these stories, I also wanted to highlight what God was orchestrating in the middle. When I first started writing, like I mentioned in the first chapter, there were stories still vivid in memory, like they happened yesterday. Justice in history class was one of those, and the other was the Los Gatos coffee shop. I found myself processing more through those stories each time I'd go back to read and edit, ensuring that the most vulnerable truth was written for you. What I didn't yet know or understand was why. Why is it that those stories still matter to me after all these years?

Every few months, I take the girls down to visit my folks on their horse ranch. I didn't grow up there, but it's like reliving childhood watching my kids ride and run free. One evening, after I put them down for bed, I joined mom and dad for a glass of wine and the latest episode American Ninja Warrior. We'd chat during commercial breaks and as I filled them in on the status of this book, I mentioned my history teacher and laughed that it's what I used to lead this narrative. My dad asked to be reminded of that teacher's name, and as I said it, my mom put her phone down and their eyes got weirdly large. You guys, this now retired teacher has become a fundamental part of the fundraisers for my parents' non-profit. We've since connected and when he introduced me to his girlfriend at my folks' fundraiser, he said, *This is the one who challenged me and left a mark.* I would have placed bets on him forgetting that by now. And then we line danced because what is life when God brings that person back as you wrap up final edits?

A few weeks before Christmas, I noticed a familiar name on social media. God bless the gram. She had commented on a mutual friend's post, so I went bold and requested to follow her. We hadn't spoken much since the coffee shop and I was sure she still held some kind of grudge but I hoped I was wrong. Within the hour she accepted my request and what started out as dwee-da-lee dialogue in messaging led to FaceTime. We introduced our children and after an hour or so of reconnecting, I asked for forgiveness for not loving her well and I shared my experience with her. There were no long blinks this time.

    I could not have imagined, in a thousand suns, that God would provide the opportunity for restoration with her. I would not believe you if, after high school graduation, someone told me I'd line dance with that teacher almost eighteen years later. And then it happens and I see the clouds parting open to the majesty of the heavens, with the full promises of God displayed. And why? Because He is so, so good, friends. He not only provides restoration and forgiveness, but also allows for humor and relief. Be patient with yourself and with your story. The kind of patience you use while you're helping to teach your kids to read. When you sit on the edge of their bed, white-knuckling the mattress as it takes thirty-eight minutes to get through one page of the chapter book they insisted on starting just before bedtime. Give yourself that kind of patience, whether it's the first day of healing or the three-thousandth.

This is not a book to steer your politics or faith. It's simply to share my story because I believe that God has provided the opportunity to do so. I hesitated a little on the title of **The "A" Words** mostly because it's just there for the taking. I wasn't sure if it alluded to curiosity or offensiveness, but the more I wrote, the more accurate that title and the theme became. It's what it is. In plain view. I think it's where God wanted me to be all along, in the light of these stories. Neither abuse or abortion are dessert and port conversations but maybe the port would help. These topics suggest controversy and stigmas. They overstep boundaries of the simple relationships. In Knox McCoy's book, *The Wondering Years*, he says this:

> *Eventually we all have to decide if the things we believe work within the larger patchwork of our lives, right? My dad calls is*

situational ethics. You believe stealing is wrong, but if you could steal and no one would be hurt and no one would find out, would you do it? If you would steal, then you probably never really believed in the wrongness of it in the first place, just the shame that would come with potentially getting caught. In the same way, I agreed with the notion that my faith was important, but actually practicing and prioritizing it? I was less enthused about that.

The shallowness of my faith was exposed post-abortion and it had very little to do with the actual abortion. It had everything to do with the notion that I wasn't forgiven. Over the years of my pain playing captive to darkness, everything I believed about myself and God was in question. Was God actually as good as I heard He was? Did His goodness extend to me? And then He asked me to share my story and it wasn't just for that friend of a friend. It was for me. It was the very heart of Romans 8:28 playing out for me- *all things* were working for good because I am His. His goodness showed up in every conversation, even the hard ones that kept me waiting, even in the ones that sorted and secured friendships. Today I look back and out, over and under the years and moments prior to writing this book and I am in tears. The faith I questioned was circumstantial based on the hardness of enduring abuse, panic and my own choices against the confidence of who I was becoming. It had nothing to do with the truth that God really is who He says, because believe it or not, I don't have the power to determine His Sovereignty. The ultimate release begins with and in God. It is an astounding thing to be loved by such a great King.

APPRECIATION

I don't think words will ever add up to the amount of gratefulness I have for you reading this. The hours spent writing and praying, researching and remembering have been worth every minute, every hour, every year and ever tear-soaked pillow because of what I believe God will do with these stories and with yours.

Thank you to my King. You give me breath and life.

Thank you, Eric, for believing with me that God is greater. Thank you for challenging me to write beyond what I thought I was capable of. Thank you for washing my feet.

Thank you to my girls: Izzy, Abby and Finley Joy. Thank you for being patient with me. Thank you for helping me with your humor and with your sisterly antics so that I had stories to share. Thank you for loving each other with conviction. You are my greatest blessings.

Thank you Mom and Dad. Your unwavering support is life. Your love is fuel.

Thank you brother. You are a pillar.

Thank you to all of my mentors, to name a few but not all, in no particular order: Debbie Hedberg, Anne Lamott, Lisa Gates, Betty Kennedy, Lisa Jo Baker, Audrey Keirstead, Jen Hatmaker, Debbie Osborn, Kathy Levering, Linda Keirstead, Lisa Kennedy, Pat McCaskey, and Hillary Brubaker.

Thank you to women and men everywhere telling your stories. Thank you for standing in the cross-fire to ensure that others know their value.

Thank you to my girls, near and far. You are treasured and sacred and holy and I appreciate every single one of you.

Thank you to my small group over the last ten years. You are a gift of great loyalty, challenge, promise and hope. I completely believe that God has called us all together for specific seasons and a purpose beyond what we can ever know. We have been there with each other through the grief of losing loved ones and through divorce, witnessed one another's work and educational successes and held each other's wee babies at birth. Each of you, past and present, have played an instrumental role in my faith and in my greater story. Thank you.

Vicky, thank you for watching my girls so that I could focus on these stories. You deserve one million dollars and a beach vacation.

Madi. Oh my dear, wonderful and talented Madi. Thank you for figuring this out with me. Thank you for being patient with me and seeing the vision in each edit. You are a work of genius.

Articles and Aids

A Spark of Light by Jodi Picoult
Bird by Bird by Anne Lamott
Finding Karishma by Bob Goff
In Our Backyard by Nita Belles
It's Not Supposed To Be This Way by Lysa TerKeurst
Out of the Spin Cycle by Jen Hatmaker
Parenting With Love and Logic by Foster Cline and Jim Fray
Sheet Music by Dr. Kevin Leman
The Danish Way of Parenting by Jessica Joelle Alexander and Iben Sandahl
The Gift of Failure by Jessica Lahey
We Saved You A Seat by Lisa Jo Baker
When I Pray For You (kids book) by Matthew Paul Turner
Polaris Project (polarisproject.org)
Not For Sale (notforsalecampaign.org)
RAINN (rainn.org) - sexual abuse prevention
National Human Trafficking Hotline
1 (888) 373-7888

ARCHIVES

Anne Lamott: Small Victories- Spotting Improbable Moments of Grace

Anne Lamott: Traveling Mercies- Some Thoughts on Grace

Anne Lamott: Bird by Bird

C.S. Lewis: Mere Christianity

Knox McCoy: The Wondering Years

Henri Nouwen. <u>brainyquotes.com</u>

Holy Bible ESV: Genesis 6-7, Psalm 103: 4, 8, 10, 12-13, Lamentations 3:37-38, Acts 9, John 4: 9, 17-18, Romans 8:28

Jodi Picoult: A Spark Of Light

Rebecca Serle: The Dinner List

Lysa TerKeurst: It's Not Supposed To Be This Way

ABOUT ME

As I mentioned, writing these next couple of paragraphs was the hardest part of this whole book. Do I use third person? First person? Should I hire a friend to write this for me? Do I write it more like a letter to you? I've just shared the breadth of my life with you and now I only need to add a few more details to sum me up and round it out.

I'll write it in first person because it otherwise feels posed and that's just not me. I'm as basic of a white girl as there is, minus the selfie-stick. You'll usually find me in denim, either shorts or jeans, with a casual tank and hoodie or mustard cardigan. I will always want to live within 30 minutes of water. A lake, the beach, a large pond, makes no difference, just give me the water. I'm a 2 on the Enneagram scale; a helper and connector, and that's all I'll say about that. For as long as I can remember, I've been writing with dreams of publishing and traveling the world. I fully believe in the restoration that comes through Jesus alone. My husband and I are going on 10 years of marriage, raising our three honey daughters and lab, Otis, in the glory of Northern California. You can find more of my writing on the blog, lemonsinmycoffee.com where I embarrass my children with their wild stories and share how I'm learning through them.

    I'd like to also take this opportunity to let you know that I'm happily available for articles and speaking on issues of abuse, abortion, marriage and motherhood. You can contact me via Instagram, em_turner or through my blog email, lemonsinmycoffee@gmail.com.

    xo

Emily